The Atlantic Crises

Britain, Europe, and Parting from the United States

William Hopkinson

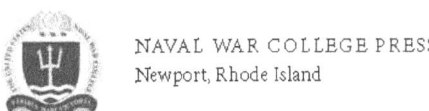

NAVAL WAR COLLEGE PRESS
Newport, Rhode Island

Naval War College

Newport, Rhode Island
Center for Naval Warfare Studies
Newport Paper Twenty-three
May 2005

President, Naval War College
Rear Admiral Jacob L. Shuford, U.S. Navy

Provost/Dean of Academics
Professor James F. Giblin, Jr.

Dean of Naval Warfare Studies
Dr. Kenneth H. Watman

Naval War College Press

Editor: Dr. Peter Dombrowski
Managing Editor: Pelham G. Boyer

Telephone: 401.841.2236
Fax: 401.841.1071
DSN exchange: 948
E-mail: press@nwc.navy.mil
Web: www.nwc.navy.mil/press

The Newport Papers are extended research projects that the editor, the dean of Naval Warfare Studies, and the President of the Naval War College consider of particular interest to policy makers, scholars, and analysts.

The views expressed in the Newport Papers are those of the authors and do not necessarily reflect the opinions of the Naval War College or the Department of the Navy.

Correspondence concerning the Newport Papers may be addressed to the editor of the Naval War College Press. To request additional copies, back copies, or subscriptions to the series, please either write the President (Code 32S), Naval War College, 686 Cushing Road, Newport, RI 02841-1207, or contact the Press staff at the telephone, fax, or e-mail addresses given.

Contents

Foreword, *by Peter Dombrowski*   v

Introduction: Why Another Book?   1

CHAPTER ONE   The Beginning:
                     The United States and Britain to 1940   9

CHAPTER TWO   The Special Relationship Grows
                     and Ends, 1940–1946   15

CHAPTER THREE   The American Half Century,
                     and European Contrasts   23

CHAPTER FOUR   The United States and Europe
                     in the Twenty-first Century   35

CHAPTER FIVE   Whither Britain?   59

CHAPTER SIX   New Relationships for Old   77

Notes   89

Abbreviations   93

Further Reading   95

About the Author   97

The Newport Papers   99

Foreword

The transatlantic relationship has come under enormous stress from both sides of the ocean since the end of the Cold War and, especially, the election of President George W. Bush. The collapse of the Warsaw Pact and the Soviet Union threw American and European strategic thought into disarray as scholars and policy makers alike scrambled to formulate new rationales for Cold War institutions like the North Atlantic Treaty Organization and the much-ballyhooed "special relationship" between the United States and the United Kingdom. Unfortunately, no one with the clear vision of the late George F. Kennan emerged to soften transatlantic squabbles over the Balkans, the post-Soviet space, and emerging security challenges in the Middle East, Africa, and Asia.

Bush administration officials and like-minded pundits miffed many Europeans with their causal unilateralist rhetoric and apparent willingness to abandon long-standing multilateral initiatives like the Kyoto Treaty. After a brief warming of relations following the horrific attacks of 11 September, American-European interactions turned sour once again as France and Germany led the effort to prevent the UN Security Council from passing a resolution authorizing the Iraq invasion. Of the major European powers only Great Britain offered substantial assistance to the American-led coalition, an artifact of Prime Minister Blair's personal commitments and perhaps of the special relationship. Today, the gradual disengagement of other European coalition members from Iraq and the reluctance of NATO to play a more active role there further fuels discontent in Washington policy circles. The 2003 announcement by Javier Solana of the European Union of a European Security Strategy rekindled American fears that the EU would either emerge as a challenger to U.S. primacy or, paradoxically, remain too weak to support American global initiatives.

Aside from the ebbs and flows of politics, the fate of the transatlantic alliance remains a major strategic question for both the United States and its various European partners. A serious, long-term breach of the close security cooperation that characterized most of the Cold and post–Cold War periods would force both sides to rethink their defense policies.

From a naval perspective, the transatlantic relationship remains one of the strategic touchstones for the American navy, even as the geostrategic focus of the United States has shifted from Europe to the Middle East and Asia. European navies—not only those of Great Britain but of France and Germany, and others as well—support American-led operations across the globe. In the Indian Ocean, for example, Europe provided ships and aircraft to enforce embargoes on material destined for Afghanistan and Iraq prior to the campaigns of 2002 and 2003. Across the globe, European allies have participated in exercises associated with the Proliferation Security Initiative.

With *The Atlantic Crises: Britain, Europe, and Parting from the United States*, Mr. William Hopkinson weighs in with a commonsensical and timely overview of the origins and evolution of the transatlantic relationship since the Second World War. He pays particular attention to the U.S. relationship with Great Britain and its impact upon intra-European debates. He reminds us that while the transatlantic relationship has never been as smooth as some would have us believe, common interests and values have allowed all parties to adjust, and readjust, to changes in the security environment and particular national goals. However, and perhaps most importantly, Hopkinson recognizes that the current breach may be far more serious than those of the past and thus that greater efforts may be required to reach accommodations in the future.

Mr. Hopkinson is especially well placed to comment wisely on transatlantic relations. He served at senior levels in the British Ministry of Defence navigating the shoals between Great Britain, the United States, and the Continent. Since leaving government he has thought and written extensively at several of the finest think tanks in Europe, including Chatham House and the Stockholm International Peace Research Institute, publishing a series of well-thought-of analyses of contemporary security issues. We at the Naval War College Press are pleased to be able to publish this important look at the past, present, and future of one of the most important strategic issues facing the United States.

PETER DOMBROWSKI
Editor, Naval War College Press
Newport, Rhode Island

Introduction: Why Another Book?

Europa, meantime, could see no end to this crazy sea crossing. But she guessed what would happen to her when they hit land again. . . . The bull knelt down in front of her, offering her his back. And the moment she climbed up, he made a dash for the sea.

It would in any case have been desirable to review the transatlantic relationship more than a decade after the end of the Cold War, taking account of the interlinked processes of globalization and a changing security agenda. The events of 11 September 2001 and the publication of the U.S. national security strategy in September 2002 reinforced the need. A review was made imperative by the fissures opened up within Western alliance and security structures, as well as globally, by the action of the United States and United Kingdom against Iraq, and arguably the requirement was further reinforced by the reelection of President George W. Bush in November 2004. Whatever the longer-term outcome of that reelection and of Iraq, transatlantic relations have changed, as have intra-European ones. It is time, especially for Britain, to think hard about what has happened and what the next steps should be.

The British, and in large measure other (Western) Europeans, have acquiesced in a form of U.S. hegemony for at least the greater part of half a century. Politicians have spoken and acted as if the transatlantic relationship of the post-1950 period, whatever it was, would endure for all time. However, Europe itself, collectively and as individual nations, has changed out of all recognition since 1950. Meanwhile, since 1990, the very nature of security, and hence of international relations, has also changed radically, and the changes have been reinforced by the American reaction to the newly perceived vulnerability of the United States. New issues, new perceptions, new actors, and new ways of acting all point to the need to revisit transatlantic relations and the various relationships embraced by the term, not in any hostile spirit but to see what the best course for everyone may be.

That will not be easy for Britain, for which a false consciousness of recent history and transatlantic relations is a particular problem. There is a widely held belief there that the relationship with the United States is special and enduring. That has been constantly reinforced by various issues in domestic politics and by Prime Minister Tony Blair's having made it a fundamental plank of his policy. In an address to British ambassadors in January 2003 he stated that the first principle of British foreign policy is that the country should remain the closest ally of the United States. That begs several questions: firstly, whether the United Kingdom is in fact the closest ally of the United States; secondly, why it should be in Britain's interest to do what may be necessary to retain that position; and thirdly, whether there is scope for an enduring principle of that sort, it not being in the sole gift of Britain to make itself anyone else's closest ally.

In Europe more generally, there are a variety of opinions about transatlantic relationships. There is less talk of a "special relationship," but there is often a facile extrapolation of some selected security facts of the Cold War into a very different era (often while other more enduring matters are neglected). While some countries, such as France, seek, or purport to seek, a degree of thought and action independent from the United States, others, particularly but not only smaller states in Eastern Europe, feel that continued American engagement in their security is vital and would be content in essence were the United States to retain the sort of leading role that it properly played until 1991. However, even for these states, American unwillingness to do what it did before, in the manner in which it used to do it, means that a review of relationships is necessary.

Inhabiting the same world, and with much political, social, and economic background in common, Americans and Western Europeans in particular obviously face many of the same problems internationally and even domestically. However, facing common problems is not necessarily the same thing as having common interests; even if interests are common, perceptions of interests may differ markedly. Moreover, even if there be agreement on interests and their perception, there may be significant divergences on how they may best be pursued, for even with much common background, American and European values are not identical. Americans and Europeans attach different weights to the utility and morality of military force; they have different views about the role of the state and of safety nets for the less fortunate members of society. In the international sphere, they differ markedly over national sovereignty and the degree to which it may or should be limited by international law and international institutions.[1]

All that said, anyone who emphasizes the need to engage with the United States must be in some sense correct. It is a superpower economically, militarily, and politically, and its size and singularity are matters that are or should be of prime concern to all other states. No country can ignore the impact of the United States in international affairs. That must be particularly true of those countries, and groups of countries, that have global interests of whatever kind. The European Union (EU) already has global economic interests and is developing widespread political concerns. Some of its members, particularly the United Kingdom and France, are global actors, albeit on a much smaller scale than the United States.

The United Kingdom has global interests and a permanent seat on the United Nations Security Council; it is a significant member of the EU and plays a major role in European security structures, of which the most important to date has been NATO. For British diplomacy, irrespective of Mr. Blair's formulation of policy, relations with the United States, both bilateral and as a member of the EU, will continue to be a major concern in a variety of ways and at several levels. Nevertheless, the relationship as it has been understood for the last half century or so will not continue unchanged, and nor should it. There have already been some significant shifts, and more may be expected. That will be true of both the special relationship and, even if that latter should not exist, the more general one.

Western Europe as a whole was able to recover after the Second World War and to develop its political and economic structures only because of the involvement of the United States in safeguarding the region from the threat of Soviet attack or subversion. For Britain, the United States has been a major market for exports, a major area for overseas investment, and the provider of technology and inward investment. Moreover, the transatlantic relationship has been a major factor in British domestic politics for most of the postwar era. Relations with the United States, as well as being of significance themselves, tend to be a defining factor, being seen by some as the obverse of relations with the EU and of commitments to Europe. For other European countries the transatlantic relationship has been important in somewhat different ways.

As regards Britain, at the start of the twentieth century, after difficult or distant relations with the United States in the nineteenth, there was talk of "Anglo-Saxendom," of the future of the Anglo-Saxon peoples. That did not long endure; there was little substance to it, except that one world power and a potential world power spoke the same language. That last was not a trivial fact, but it did not make for a substantial political bond. It certainly did not take away the normal frictions and clash of interests of two different nations. Not until the very end of the 1930s at the earliest was there anything that could justify the term "special relationship." Such a relationship did indeed come into existence in the course of the Second World War, but even then, on both sides, the basis, quite properly, was interest, not charity or benevolence. Initially, there was a partnership of equals; indeed in many areas—military, technical, intelligence—Britain was the leading player. However, roles were mostly reversed within quite a short time, and by the end of the war the United States was undoubtedly the more significant partner.

Winston Churchill was by then striving to make an enduring relationship of a special nature but in general was not succeeding.

As regards the rest of Europe, only from about 1950 was there real substance to talk of a wider transatlantic community, one in which there were major shared interests and underlying political and economic cement. The foundations were laid in the Marshall Plan and then consolidated in the Atlantic Alliance. Thereafter, and throughout the Cold War, U.S. engagement in Europe was, and was generally seen to be, absolutely necessary to preserve the interests of both sides.[2] However, there is now no need to confront or deter a heavily armed opponent based far forward in Europe. The Soviet Union has gone; communism is no longer an ideological challenge but almost universally perceived as a gross failure. The urgent task is to integrate Russia and the other successor states and the liberated nations of the East into Europe and indeed into wider international society. That effort certainly will greatly benefit from U.S. engagement, but that will not be engagement of the sort required from 1949 to 1989. Meanwhile, the new security threats, principally global terrorism, require very different means and different collaborators to address them. In some important aspects the Europeans can contribute proportionately much more to dealing with those threats than they did to Soviet containment, while for a variety of reasons the United States in practice contributes much less to it than it did to the old agenda.

In part, this Newport Paper is an attempt to provide a basis for thinking about how transatlantic relations now stand. In part, it is an attempt to think how they could and should be. Finally it is in part an attempt to peer into the future. Ideally, one would wish to look forty years ahead, just a working lifetime, to reflect on where some of the current changes we see about us might lead. However, it is extremely difficult to see so far ahead; indeed, it is difficult to take a twenty-year span. If the aim of the monograph may be expressed briefly, it is that the Europeans in general, the British in particular (given past history and perceptions), the Americans, and the world community (whatever that may be) should all reflect on the relationships between the United States and European nations, individually and collectively, to try to understand better how they may be improved, and as a preliminary to that, what their objectives are as regards those relationships.

This work does not seek to be an original work of scholarship in the sense of being based in its historical parts on archival research; to establish the facts and the narrative of the history of American relations with Europe and with Britain up to and beyond the Second World War it depends on work done by others. It does not seek to rehearse the whole history of U.S.-British collaboration in the Second World War, nor the entire course of the Cold War. It touches on sufficient of the former to give an understanding of how what is called the "special relationship" came about, and how difficult and fraught it was even in the closest days; it sketches out salient factors from the latter aspect to give a feel for what the North Atlantic alliance was about, the underlying community of interests in resisting communism (the main U.S. concern) and Soviet threats (the European one).

Such claim to originality as the monograph has rests on the analysis of what the historical facts indicate and of what courses might best serve the interests of the United Kingdom and of other European nations. Such matters are questions of judgment; different inferences may legitimately be drawn as to the likely course of future events. At the least, however, such inferences should be drawn unencumbered by a false understanding of what has happened in the past and of what the earlier motivations of the actors may have been.

The approach is very much that of traditional international relations, but from an applied, or practitioner's, viewpoint, not that of theory. There will be no postmodern discourse! What is intended, in effect, is to ask readers to set themselves an examination paper with a number of questions. It would have been good if politicians could have sat such an exam by the time of the recent British election so that the government had some of the answers. They did not, and the government shows little sign of being aware of the problems.

The most significant manifestation of the transatlantic relationship for some fifty years was the Atlantic Alliance. That is still sometimes referred to in terms like the "bedrock of European security." It may perhaps be such, but more probably it is not. The question needs to be asked and, to the extent possible, answered. At the very least, both that alliance and the transatlantic relationship have altered, and they continue to alter. Some would argue the need to renew or refresh them. Some might argue for scrapping them. The issues rather are what the challenges are that face Europeans and Americans at the start of the twenty-first century, how they can best be met, and what implications that has for how the United States, individual European states, and Europeans collectively should conduct themselves.

From those comes a more detailed list of questions addressing such matters as:

- What is the U.S. interest now in Europe?
- How does that interest compare in nature and importance with its interests in other places, and its domestic concerns?
- What is the United States likely to *wish* to do to meet its interests?
- What is the United States *willing* to do or give to meet its interests?
- What are the regional and global interests of the United Kingdom and Europe?
- What should Europeans be doing globally, given their interests and capabilities or potential capabilities?

- How far are U.S. interests—security, economic, and political—compatible with British and European interests?

- How far is the United States willing to meet those interests, and how are conflicts of interest likely to be resolved?

In short, the fundamental question of transatlantic relations (taking them to include all the particular, individual, and special relationships) is to what extent the two sides can be *ad idem* as to ends and means. Two opposed players may certainly have relations, usually bad ones. Transatlantic ones, however, are said to be beneficial, special, vital, etc. It is necessary to ask whether this is true for both sides of the Atlantic, and if so, why. If it is not, then what does each bring to its relationships, what does each seek, and what does each get from them? A further dimension of all that is whether the price exacted by or from either party could be incommensurate with the benefits bestowed. Even if the balance is positive, it is still necessary to consider whether it will remain so, given the likely flow of costs and benefits.

In attempting answers it is above all necessary to see the world as it really is, not through spectacles, however venerable their original maker or comfortable their fit. Great men may indeed give guidance of enduring value, but they cannot be expected to have foreseen all the changes of the last fifty years, let alone the last two centuries. For Britons the perspective on the transatlantic relationship is often very much that of the Churchill of the Second World War. That perspective, however valid at the time, needs to be set against Churchill's own earlier judgments and against subsequent history.

Each reader will have to make his or her own attempt at assessing the situation. A preliminary overall judgment, however, would be that the United States and the European democracies still have a great deal in common in terms of liberal values, a belief in human rights and freedoms, and a generally open view of economic matters. American relations with Europe are, as a whole, much better than those with other parts of the world, even allowing for the tensions that arose in the first few months of 2003. There is obviously much that the United States and Europeans can and should do together. However, the relationship cannot be the old one as established in the 1950s.

The United States may be indispensable in the sense that its size and economic weight must be part of the management of world affairs, political and economic, but it is not uniquely wise; it does not demonstrate perfect understanding of the appropriate solutions to a variety of problems. On the contrary, it shows unilateral tendencies that make more difficult a joint approach with the Europeans (and others) to many issues that would benefit from a common engagement. Above all, except on the solely military measure, great as is the weight of the United States, it is not the greater part of the world. It has to understand that military hegemony will not solve the global problems confronting it.

For their part, the Europeans have much to do to pull themselves together politically and militarily. Until both sides of the Atlantic address their deficiencies, the two together will not be able to make the impact upon world affairs that their economic strength and collective abilities would justify. A new relationship could do much more to improve global security; it would also serve better the interests of the European players and probably, in the long term, those of the United States itself.

Washington feels understandable frustration at the unwillingness of European players to follow its lead, acknowledge the contribution that America makes to world security, and get their act together politically and militarily. The Americans might also be forgiven for thinking the Europeans ungrateful for what has been done for them in the past and shortsighted about the dangers of the future. There is good deal in all that, particularly the last part. However, there is another side to the story.

American engagement in Europe from the 1940s served U.S. ends. There was a vital national interest in preserving Western Europe from aggression or subversion. Moreover, that engagement brought great influence over European foreign and defense policies, producing a band of loyal allies. So, while there may be complaints about what each party gave and received in the past, one can safely say that all benefited, and at a generally very moderate cost. For the future, the equations are more difficult. The United States will be required to put in much less to European security; the Europeans will benefit much less from American engagement of the sort that one saw in the second half of the twentieth century. Taking a wide view, what can and should each side of the Atlantic now expect from the other? What are the potential benefits and costs of collaboration; what are the potential losses and costs should they fail to collaborate?

For the United Kingdom, with its asserted special relationship, the same questions arise, but in even more pointed and difficult form, not least because the issues become entangled in domestic politics. Moreover, the United Kingdom needs to consider just what, if anything, constitutes that special relationship and how much it is prepared to pay for it, not only vis-à-vis the United States but also as regards Europe. It needs, too, to reflect on whether the long-standing assertion that it must never be placed in a position of having to choose between Europe and the United States remains or can remain true. Even more importantly, it may need to consider whether, even if it does not in fact have to make such a choice, it needs to rid itself of a false consciousness that suggests that any choice is an exclusive one between a permanent overall commitment to Washington and pursuing its interests in Europe—a decision that any country might wish to avoid. Britain has, on occasion, certainly neglected what it ought to have done in and with Europe because of a desire to avoid a difference with the United States. Obviously, no British government would wish to forego the benefits it gains from the transatlantic military and intelligence relationship; however, the United States remains in that relationship because it believes that it too gains thereby. Would it forego the benefits of that relationship merely because the British government has aligned itself with European partners on some issue? Would it remain in the relationship, no matter how often the United Kingdom had foregone a European option, if America did not benefit from it? (It may be, of course, that Washington's gain from that relationship is the general alignment of London with it; if so, that should be faced head-on in considering the benefits and costs to the United Kingdom.)

The wider global community has much to gain from a positive and balanced transatlantic relationship. However, it is that wider community that has least opportunity to formulate policies, or even thinking, on that. The General Assembly of the UN is not the ideal forum for the weighing and discussion of arguments that relate to that sort of thing. In any case, even though the earlier, foolish, anticolonialism has abated and there is no Soviet-U.S. conflict to add oil to the flames, there is sufficient disgruntled reaction to globalization and to the Western approach to a range of issues, economic and security related, to make it unlikely that there would be a general public acknowledgment in the General Assembly of the benefits that can and should flow from rich, liberal states cooperating on the international stage. Nevertheless, human rights, development, and resolution of disputes could all benefit from transatlantic cooperation.

Moreover, the great questions of Islam and modernity, as well as of the integration of Russia and China into the wider international system, could all be helped by an effective relationship between the United States and the major European players. That would certainly need significant changes on both sides of the Atlantic, changes of which the players may not be capable. Even so, however, the attempt should be made to understand what is and what might be, even if the latter is not attainable in practice.

CHAPTER ONE

The Beginning
The United States and Britain to 1940

Even after the radical changes in immigration and ethnic composition of the twentieth century, the United States is still recognizably the child of Europe. It may have out-grown its parent, moved away, and be determined to go its own way in life, but its constitution and values still reflect its ancestry. They are largely British, indeed English, but also, both through the English heritage and directly, with an admixture of Christian and Enlightenment Europe. A century ago there were those who saw the United States as a part of Anglo-Saxendom, and even later it was seen as an essentially Protestant country. The former could not be said today (and in this era of political correctness would not be said—except by those of a French turn of phrase seeking to contrast certain free market tendencies with another more state or society-centric tradition). However, in its machinery of government, its law, even much of the spirit animating its politics, the line of descent is not only obvious but still of practical importance. The Protestant point is more difficult—it is clearly true in that the Christian Right in the United States is a formidable force in politics, up to the highest levels. However, there are strong tendencies and other traditions there that make the country very different from what have traditionally been thought of as the Protestant countries of Europe, such as Sweden or the Netherlands, or Scotland; also, the Protestantism of the U.S. Right has little in common with the Methodism of England or the Lutheranism of Germany.

English common law—the rights established, or thought to have been established, in medieval and early modern England, and especially in the settlement after the struggles of the seventeenth century (the Glorious Revolution)—was the basis on which most early American political thinking and much political action was based. Obviously the political break at the American Revolution led not only to a change in the rule over the former colonies but in some cases by the colonials to efforts to emphasize that their system and habits were not British. Moreover, the early decades of the new republic saw political debates on what were essentially new issues such as states' rights as against the federal institutions. Nevertheless, most of the antecedents of U.S. political and legal structures could (and can) be traced back to Britain, and economic and trading ties were still of major importance. Talleyrand was able even as soon after the American Revolution as 1796 to write that the country (where he had lived since 1794) was at heart English and that it was England more than any other country that stood to bene-fit from the rapidly increasing prosperity and population of its former colonists. (In due course Bismarck was to assert that the fact that the United States and the British Empire spoke the same language was of fundamental importance for the future.)

A common language did not, of course, prevent the United States and Britain going to war in 1812 or forestall a variety of tensions right up to the end of the nineteenth cen-tury. Some of those derived from disputes over the border with Canada. Others in-volved territorial issues in which the United States had no interest of its own but was desirous of putting pressure on Britain, as when in 1895 it informed Britain that the latter should submit to arbitration its dispute with Venezuela over the boundaries of British Guiana. That application of the Monroe Doctrine was accompanied by the as-sertion that "today the United States is practically sovereign on this continent"—an al-most breathtaking assertion of imperium from a supposedly nonimperial power.[1] Yet other disagreements derived from political tension unrelated to boundaries, such as the revision in 1901 of the Clayton-Bulwer Treaty of 1850 (on the isthmian canal) and, be-fore that, problems that arose from British actions during the U.S. Civil War. In short, during most of the nineteenth century, there was nothing very warm or special in Anglo–U.S. interstate relations; only at the very end was a new development perceptible.

From the 1890s, there was an appreciation in Britain that the world order, under which there had been unprecedented economic growth, could no longer be sustained by Brit-ish seapower alone. Despite the jingoism triggered by the Venezuelan incident, there was a degree of rapprochement between the United States and the United Kingdom over the decade up to 1904, and this was perhaps a factor in decisions, taken on wider grounds, by which strategically Britain was to abandon the Western Hemisphere. There was still an undercurrent of thinking in the U.S. Navy that envisaged the possibility of war with Britain (and this was to resurface later), but the more general attitude was that interests were likely to be shared.

More generally, the founding fathers of the U.S. republic envisaged peaceful contact and commerce with all nations but entangling alliances with none. (The original treaty with France was in effect dead by 1793, and the Jay Treaty of 1794, while an accommo-dation with British interests, was not an entangling alliance.) The founders' vision shaped much of the country's foreign policy through the nineteenth century. Trade, inward invest-ment, and emigration ensured a great deal of contact between the United States and Eu-rope. However, there was nothing that could be called a special transatlantic relationship except for the ties of commerce and language with the United Kingdom, and de facto dependence on the Royal Navy for the effectiveness of the Monroe Doctrine.

At the end of the nineteenth century the United States went to war with Spain, but that was essentially a Western Hemisphere matter. Early in the new century it at first contrived to keep out of the Great War (the First World War), coming in only when its shipping suffered from unrestricted submarine warfare. It did not integrate its military efforts (as opposed to some extent its naval ones) with its allies, and it bore only a late and small (albeit important) part of the fighting. At the end, the United States played a major role in the peace negotiations and the shaping of postwar Europe but then failed to ratify the treaty establishing the League of Nations, in the formulation of which it had been the prime mover.

Between the two world wars, the United States did not engage greatly in European affairs—there was no distinguishable transatlantic relationship. U.S.-British relations were generally reserved. American military planners still considered war between the two countries possible up to the 1930s; for their part, in the 1930s the British made the assumption that there would be no war with the United States in the next ten years, hardly an assumption that relations were so close and special that war was inconceivable.[2] There was clear recognition in British circles that a friendly attitude from the United States was by no means to be relied on. In 1927 Churchill, then Chancellor of the Exchequer, commented that while it was undoubtedly right, in the interests of peace, to go on talking about war with the United States as unthinkable, everyone knew that it was not true.[3] However disastrous such a war would be, Britain would not wish to put itself into the power of the United States and could not tell what they might do if they were in a position to give orders about British policy in India, Egypt, or Canada. The same year, the Foreign Office commented, "We have treated them too much as blood relations, not sufficiently as a foreign country." In 1928 the secretary of the cabinet noted that Britain had conceded to the United States over the League of Nations, the Japanese alliance, naval armaments, debt settlement, and Ireland. Britain, he lamented, was always making concessions and was always being told that the next step would change the U.S. attitude. However, the United States only became more overbearing and suspicious than ever.

It may be sufficient to round out this catalogue of official assessment with the views of the head of the Foreign Office in 1932: "We have been too tender, not to say subservient, with the United States for a long time past. . . . It is still necessary, and I desire as much as ever, that we should get on well with this untrustworthy race. But we shall never get very far: they will always let us down." Whether or not Neville Chamberlain would have expressed matters in quite that form, the case is that his own dealings with the United States from about this time (as Chancellor of the Exchequer) proceeded on the basis of a far from friendly view of that country.

Economic relations and tariffs were one source of friction; however, probably the major source of tension was naval rivalry. After the First World War the Royal Navy was still the larger, but the United States was determined to achieve parity, and also to end the alliance between Britain and Japan. At the 1921 Washington Conference on naval armaments, the United States proposed the ratio of 5:5:3 in major capital ships between the United States, the United Kingdom, and Japan. Extraordinarily, it also listed the names of twenty-three ships that it said the Royal Navy must give up.

Britain could not afford a naval race with the United States and acquiesced in both limitations on capital ships and the ending of its Japanese alliance. Nevertheless, new tension over naval armaments followed in 1927 at a further conference called by the United States to consider smaller ships. With a worldwide empire to protect and extensive trade routes upon which the country was absolutely dependent, Britain was in a position in no sense symmetrical with that of the United States. Britain sought the right to seventy cruisers but in 1930 agreed that the 5:5:3 ratio should apply to cruisers as well, with a limit of fifty of these ships for the Royal Navy.

Despite quarrels with Britain in the nineteenth century, there had been little U.S. clamor against the British Empire. Not until the twentieth century, when the United States itself was or was becoming a global power, did this particular source of friction become important. The watershed was around the time of the First World War, after the fading of the feelings about Anglo-Saxendom. There became manifest in the interwar period, and indeed in some ways up to the last quarter of the twentieth century, a U.S. antagonism to the Empire as such. In part the hostility stemmed from a category mistake, confusing twentieth-century colonies with the pre-Revolutionary arrangements in America that had been so forcefully rejected at independence (and around and about which many myths had been fostered as part of U.S. nation building). In part, it was a reflection of the naval rivalry. In part it was an economic struggle—there was a strong desire to open up the Empire to U.S. trade and to remove a commercial rival.[4] This last showed itself most uncompromisingly in the post–Second World War negotiations on financial institutions, where all J. M. Keynes's eloquence could not win greater accommodation for the battered condition of the British economy and the burdens upon it.

The anticolonial posture was just about hidden at the time of the Atlantic Charter (1941) but showed itself in pressure on Churchill to advance Indian self-rule during the war. It became glaringly manifest at the time of Suez (1956); the United States then sought to distance itself from the old colonial powers in order to appear more attractive in the Third World as the Cold War competition with the Soviet Union spread to

Asia and Africa. It continued through to the 1970s in the pressure to reach a settlement in Rhodesia, when the chief American concern was to appear more attractive than the Soviet Union to rising African nationalists.

Some of the anticolonialism was understandable in the sense of the changing world; some of it was the normal reaction of one power seeking to diminish the potential of a possible rival. The latter, however, does not fit with any picture of a uniquely generous relationship with Britain—the United States, like any other power pursued its own interests. It was not wholly successful in its judgments as to what would best serve those; for example, it underestimated the instability, and consequent potential advantage to the Soviet Union, generated by the early and rapid dissolution of the old empires, as well as by the weakness of Britain—for instance, in the loss of its power to support Greece and Turkey.

Great-power rivalry aside, in the 1930s U.S. international economic policy (in particular its protectionism) was largely destructive and American international security policy largely ineffectual (for example, Washington would not apply effective sanctions to Italy after the invasion of Abyssinia). Indeed, none of the major powers comes out of the period very well: Britain declined to support either the U.S. appeal in 1931 to condemn Japanese aggression or Franklin D. Roosevelt's suggestion of a peace conference in 1938 following Hitler's threatening behavior, and France was not an effective actor.[5] Nevertheless, by the end of the decade Roosevelt was clear about the menace from Germany and was starting to talk informally about providing practical help to Britain in the event of war.[6] On Churchill's return to office at the outbreak of war, Roosevelt invited Churchill to keep in touch personally. However, there was little response to Churchill's messages, and neutrality still enjoyed very strong support in the United States. Meanwhile, the stopping and searching of American vessels by the Royal Navy provoked much friction, as it had done in the Revolutionary and Napoleonic wars and in the early years of the First World War.

In May 1940 the British War Cabinet concluded that if France fell prospects of final victory would be largely dependent on American cooperation. It was by no means clear when, or indeed if, that would be forthcoming. Even if it were, there was nothing before 1940 to suggest that there would be an enduring relationship marked by any particular friendliness between the United Kingdom and the United States. From 1939 there was the start of something that might be called a special relationship, but no more than a start. Only with the agreement of the destroyers-for-bases deal in August 1940 was there a concrete aspect to that, a development that led on quite rapidly to Lend-Lease and a remarkable degree of intelligence cooperation. Those actions marked a real entanglement of the United States in transatlantic affairs, but the country finally entered the Second World War only when it was itself attacked. Even then, it was not clear that there would in the future be anything special about U.S. relations with Europe as a whole, as opposed to other parts of the world. Only the Soviet threat and the consequent U.S. security commitment to Europe gave rise to what is recognizable as a general transatlantic relationship in the sense in which that term has been commonly used in the last fifty years or so. In the light of earlier experience, it was not clear that there would even *be* any enduring special relationship with Britain.

Churchill saw his country as having an assured seat at the top table, and he believed that a relationship between the United States and the British Empire would be a highly desirable feature of the postwar world. There is no indication that either Roosevelt or Harry Truman thought in such terms, despite Churchill's emphasis on the closeness and specialness of the relationship, both in public and in his private correspondence. Common language and culture and economic ties counted for something, but memories, accurate or inaccurate, about the circumstances that had led to independence, and clashes of interest, economic or other, counted for at least as much at the other side of the scale. Misty visions of Anglo-Saxendom had been short-lived and did not extend beyond the First World War—at any rate, until revived in rather different form by Churchill. It was he who made, out of dire necessity, what he and subsequent British politicians saw as a special relationship, and out of what might have been foreseen as a temporary relationship what promised to him to be an enduring one.

As regards Europe more generally, while some argued that American engagement from 1917 had been to save Europe from itself (an argument heard more, and more credibly, after the Second World War), there was no serious suggestion before the 1940s that continuing U.S. engagement was essential for European security. In the 1930s it was seen, especially by France, as desirable, but its absence did not preclude the forming of alliances and security arrangements that it was assumed would work without American involvement. Certainly, the French would have welcomed such engagement in the interwar years, but the idea that the European powers could not conduct their own security policies, and were not in fact the main world actors, dates only from after 1943. The necessity for U.S. involvement arose at a particular time for particular reasons; it is not a law of nature, essential though it was, or indeed may be in some future circumstance.

CHAPTER TWO

The Special Relationship Grows and Ends, 1940–1946

Following the Battle of Britain, there was growing support in the United States for Britain, and Roosevelt continued to do all that he could, short of war, to help with the provision of materiel and in other ways.[1] After his election victory in 1940, the destroyers-for-bases deal was followed at the beginning of 1941 by Lend-Lease, by an exceptional degree of collaboration on intelligence, and by preliminary staff talks.[2] In such military and intelligence cooperation lay the genesis, and lies the essence, of what became known, in Britain at any rate, as the "special relationship." The fact that this had its origins in war gave it certain characteristics that still mark what is distinctive about U.S.-British relations. These embrace military ties, intelligence, and, sometimes, a certain synergy at the highest policy levels.

Lend-Lease was devised by Roosevelt in response to an approach from Churchill in December 1940. Essentially the United States undertook to lend the supplies urgently required against postwar payment. Churchill was to describe this as the most unsordid act in the history of any nation. Nevertheless, it came with terms that he himself felt were humiliating—not only the sale of assets in the United States but the handing over of the gold reserves in Cape Town as interim measures until the bill passed into law in March 1941. However, at that stage, Averell Harriman, appointed to coordinate assistance in London, was instructed to "recommend everything we can do, short of war, to keep the British Isles afloat."

Even before that the intelligence relationship had started to grow. From Churchill's becoming prime minister he had taken steps to coordinate British intelligence operations *in* the United States. His agent for that, William Stephenson, was also to establish an entirely new degree of intelligence cooperation *with* the United States. Roosevelt agreed to his collaborating with the Federal Bureau of Investigation, under J. Edgar Hoover. With Hoover's consent, Stephenson recruited a large network of agents, and the FBI acted on the information provided by them on Axis activities. However, the very scope of these activities provoked a reaction; the assistant secretary of state commented that Stephenson was rapidly developing a full-size secret police and intelligence service. That did not lead to a diminution in the British activities, and in fact in 1941 Stephenson's role as British security coordinator was formally recognized. Indeed he went farther, attempting to maneuver to have a (named) coordinator of all U.S. intelligence appointed; his efforts bore fruit in June 1941, when following the appointment of William Donovan to coordinate U.S. overseas intelligence Stephenson was able to report: "You can imagine how relieved I am . . . that our man is in a position of such importance for our efforts."[3]

This coup, not surprisingly, had an adverse effect upon Stephenson's relations with the FBI. Hoover resented his playing politics in the bureau's own backyard, and playing them effectively. Nevertheless, security cooperation continued, and there was some pooling of military intelligence.[4]

Liaison on Britain's materiel requirements before the United States was formally at war included exchanges of scientific information with, inter alia, the transfer of knowledge and activity westward across the Atlantic. The first serious exchanges of militarily useful scientific information took place in the autumn of 1940. A British delegation was instructed to tell the Americans everything that Britain was doing in the scientific field. This included work on radar, jet engines, nuclear fission, and antisubmarine warfare. The U.S. Office of Scientific Research later called this the most valuable cargo ever brought to American shores.

The military potential of atomic energy had been realized at about the beginning of the war. Albert Einstein had written to Roosevelt on it in 1939. By mid-1941 the British were convinced that it would be possible to make a uranium bomb of enormous power. However, they also realized that they could not devote sufficient resources to explore all the potential avenues; accordingly the Ministry of Defence proposed that laboratory and design work should continue in Britain but that development of a full-scale plant should be considered in Canada or the United States. Frederick Lindemann, Churchill's scientific adviser, urged that the plant be built in Britain or Canada, since "whosoever possesses such a plant should be able to dictate terms to the rest of the world. However much I may trust my neighbour, and depend on him, I am very much averse to putting myself completely at his mercy and would therefore not press the Americans to undertake this work."

Perhaps because of a common perception of the significance of this work, collaboration on it soon became an area of considerable difficulty; formal agreements unraveled, and not until 1958 were matters finally put onto a mutually acceptable basis.[5]

Roosevelt's adviser in the atomic area (Vannevar Bush, director of the Office of Scientific Research and Development) reported the British findings. A committee chaired by him concluded in November 1941 that a fission bomb was indeed feasible. In December Churchill agreed to a full exchange of information. Actually, Bush had originally suggested that atomic weapons should be regarded as a joint project and Roosevelt had endorsed the idea, but that approach had been deflected. Nevertheless, within months the U.S. input of resources far exceeded the British, and in June 1942, in order to preserve the British position, Churchill urged the pooling of all information, the two nations to work together and share the results equally between them. By then the U.S. position had changed, and the British were excluded from U.S. work. In August 1943 Churchill persuaded Roosevelt to lift the barriers; under the Quebec agreement arrangements were made designed to ensure full and effective collaboration between the two countries and establish a mutual veto on the use of atomic weapons. The agreement imposed some restraints on postwar commercial and industrial exploitation of atomic energy by Britain; there were also de facto restraints at the time, in British exclusion from work on plutonium (as opposed to uranium) technology and weaponization.

In consequence, Churchill was moved to return to the issue of collaboration in September 1944, by which time, as British scientists moved to the United States, work in Britain on atomic weapons had almost closed down. He and Roosevelt then initialed an agreement providing the basis for indefinite full collaboration after the war between the United States and Britain in developing atomic energy for military and commercial purposes. This mutual effort was to continue unless and until terminated by joint agreement. Nevertheless, in February 1946, the United States refused a British request for the exchange of information, and the McMahon Bill threatened to terminate almost all communication about atomic energy. A series of exchanges did not advance matters, and in August the McMahon Bill was signed into law.[6] In his memoirs Truman asserted that he could not respond to a request by Clement Attlee because of the McMahon Act.[7]

Atomic energy was not to be the only issue over which Attlee felt let down by Truman as the earlier relationship waned. In terms of immediate practical effect, the abrupt termination of Lend-Lease without consultation, announced on 21 August 1945, seven days after the end of the war with Japan, had a greater impact. Britain had been longer at war than the United States, had suffered far greater physical and material damage, and incurred a heavier burden of casualties. (British military casualties in the Second World War were 244,000 dead, to which may be added another 100,000 for the Dominions and Empire;[8] U.S. casualties were 292,000.) Attlee sent a team under Keynes to negotiate a loan to mitigate the effects of the ending of the wartime arrangements, but all Keynes's eloquence could not gain the easy terms he sought to offset the weakening of Britain's position by the years of war. After three months of hard negotiations the

British secured a loan, much hedged around with restrictive terms. These included insistence that pounds sterling should be made convertible within a year and that imperial preference end following the ratification of the Bretton Woods agreement.[9] All this hardly demonstrated a very positive special relationship.

At the time of the U.S. entry into the war all this had lain in the future. Immediately after the attack on Pearl Harbor, Churchill determined to meet Roosevelt, and he did so that month, December 1941. They then laid down the strategic outline and organizational framework for the joint conduct of the war. They agreed on a strategy of "Germany first." However, while content to give priority to the European theater, the Americans were hesitant about the British peripheral approach, which, General George C. Marshall suspected, was designed to protect their interests in the Mediterranean and in the Empire. Marshall saw North Africa as a diversion; large-scale operations there would preclude a landing in France in 1943. By the time Churchill and Roosevelt next met, in mid-1942, the U.S. military staffs were very resistant to Mediterranean operations. There were other tensions too; Marshall himself felt that there was too much anti-British feeling on the American side.

Nevertheless, Churchill and Roosevelt agreed on the concentration of land, sea, and air forces under a supreme commander in each theater. There was to be integration everywhere except in the Pacific. Moreover, overall command was centralized in the Combined Chiefs of Staff, who had oversight of general military strategy, supplies, and reinforcements. Materiel and raw materials were coordinated too. Churchill also informed Roosevelt of the extent of British penetration of German ciphers through ULTRA; in due course U.S. officers were trained in handling that closely protected intelligence, and special liaison units were established with U.S. headquarters.

A further outcome of the first post–Pearl Harbor meeting was the appointment of Field Marshal Sir John Dill to liaise with Marshall and the U.S. Chiefs of Staff. This turned out to be an outstandingly successful appointment, not least because of the friendship between Dill and Marshall that ensued. It provided the basis for close collaboration between the chiefs of staff in the conduct of the war. However, British-American military relations were not easy. Dill's successor as Chief of the Imperial General Staff, Alan Brooke, did not make a favorable impression on Marshall, nor did Marshall impress Brooke, at any rate as a strategist. In particular, Brooke thought that Marshall failed to understand the military difficulties of a landing in occupied France, which Roosevelt was anxious to see happen in 1943 in order to take pressure off the Soviet Union.[10] Nor was Brooke impressed by Dwight D. Eisenhower. Meanwhile, Admiral Ernest J. King for the U.S. Navy felt throughout that the Japanese were his prime objective and that the conduct of the war against them in the Pacific was essentially an American affair.

Even while the war with Germany was still in train, Churchill sensed the decline of British influence and the decay of the relationship that was so special to him and that he so cherished. He floated various ideas to try to counteract the tendency; for example, in May 1943 he suggested a common form of citizenship for the United States and the British Commonwealth. Such palliatives could not heal the fundamental problems. In June 1944, in a message to Roosevelt, drafted but not sent, Churchill threatened to resign over ANVIL, the plan for an Allied landing in the south of France. The disagreements that arose in connection with this operation were, indeed, the start of a new pattern of U.S.-British disputes. Before the operation the British and American chiefs of staff had rarely failed to come to eventual agreement on a major issue; after it they were rarely on the same side. Reflecting the growing discrepancy of power, the British were almost always on the losing side of these disagreements, notwithstanding Churchill's tendency to bombard Roosevelt at this time, and again in the spring of 1945, with many long messages.

The differences had started even before ANVIL. In early 1942 Roosevelt wrote to Churchill urging progress on self-government for India. That was not well received, nor was subsequent advice and comment in the same vein. More fundamental to the conduct of the war and the winning of the peace were the divisions that opened up on the handling of the Soviet Union. British-U.S. coordination there was never properly consolidated before Roosevelt's death. In March 1942 Roosevelt wrote to Churchill (using himself the words "brutally frank") that he thought he personally could handle Joseph Stalin better than either the Foreign Office or the State Department. This foreshadowed later divisions that persisted as long as Roosevelt lived. They were most manifest at the Yalta conference of February 1945. Churchill had been anxious to have two or three nights with Roosevelt in advance. The president declined, and their joint preparation was confined to a working dinner. The result was seriously impaired coordination in dealing with Stalin's objectives for Eastern Europe.

In part the problem was Roosevelt's declining health, and in part a difference of strategic view—Roosevelt wished to explore the terms on which the USSR might enter the war against Japan, terms that he discussed and settled with Stalin without even consulting Churchill. While his successor, Truman, opened with a hard line on Soviet bad faith in and over Poland, he declined Churchill's suggestion in May 1945, immediately after the end of the war in Europe, that they should meet Stalin. He insisted that nothing be done that might give the impression that they were "ganging up" on him. Truman then suggested that he himself should meet Stalin alone before any tripartite meeting.

At the end of the war, Britain still had considerable military power and political weight, and so a significant role, in Europe and elsewhere, but London was scarcely influencing the direction of American policy. U.S. decisions, most especially in the economic sphere, however, were having a great impact on the United Kingdom. Only in intelligence, where there was still at least something of a British lead, was the relationship "special."

More generally, Britain and France still saw themselves as world actors. Both had major interests in Asia and the Middle East; neither saw eye to eye with the United States on those areas. The major divisions (after Truman's policies on immigration to Palestine) were over communist China, Korea, the Middle East, and Indochina, and over the strong current of U.S. anticolonialism already manifest in Roosevelt's dealings with Churchill. (The United States deviated from that line where it judged that the need to confront communism called for a different approach. For instance, it was prepared to give France a measure of support in its Indochina wars, and had the British been keener it would have given more.)

The American frustration of the Suez intervention struck a very heavy blow indeed against Britain and France. Even before the intervention was launched, the United States had been undermining the British position in Egypt. The Americans apparently had concluded that President Gamal Abdel Nasser of Egypt was their best hope for the future, even at a time when he was turning to the Soviet Union for arms supplies (and even in the light of his apparent regret at the Axis defeat). Over Suez, the U.S. action went far beyond not supporting allies in a particular action; it actively undermined their general position and standing. The outcome was to have a direct impact in Europe as well as in the longer term, making the general Western position in the Middle East more diffi-cult.[11] In the light of Suez, Britain and France drew opposing conclusions that still have a major impact on transatlantic relations and on European security policies.

The French concluded from this episode that they could not rely on the Americans and should therefore seek to be as independent as possible in their capabilities, not least in developing a nuclear arsenal. The British concluded, in contrast, that significant mili-tary action without the support of the United States was impossible and that they and the Europeans should therefore put all effort into locking Europe and the United States together, not into independent security policies.

The divisions between the United States and the Europeans in Asia were not only over general political issues; they extended to the nature of military operations and how the military should relate to the political. Eisenhower clung to the view that nuclear weap-ons were more effective than, but not different in kind from, conventional ones; this at-titude in some senses persisted to the end of the Cold War in U.S. war-fighting doctrine, and it has returned post–11 September 2001 in some American thinking on the need for nuclear weapons to preempt other weapons of mass destruction. Likewise, in and over Korea, many of the American military—not only, though preeminently, General

Douglas MacArthur—looked to waging an all-out rather than a limited war. The British (and others) remained opposed to that, and there were significant tensions between Washington and London over the sort of war to be waged. Despite British military contributions—and their high quality, albeit relatively small scale—to the Korean War, the U.S. military did not regard the British approach as helpful.

The special relationship as Churchill conceived it was short-lived. It sprang from the exigencies of war, and as victory came into view and American resources, skills, and manpower were mobilized, the relationship was transformed. With Attlee and Truman it did not survive at all in the sense of a policy relationship at the highest levels, and when he returned to office in 1951 Churchill was unable to revive the link. In late 1953 he proclaimed in public the priority that he gave to the Anglo-American partnership, but in private, and semiprivate, he was exasperated by U.S. complacence toward the hydrogen bomb and stubborn resistance to summitry.

Following the Churchill-Roosevelt era, there was a gap of more than ten years before there was again significant personal chemistry at the highest levels, and not until the Ronald Reagan–Margaret Thatcher years was there something of the old national intimacy (it is dubious whether there was much personal intimacy on Roosevelt's side between him and Churchill, as opposed to that between Reagan and Thatcher). By then, in any case, the totally subordinate role of Britain was manifest.

Well before Suez (1956) there were significant divergences in the Middle East, not least over the events leading up to the creation of Israel. After Suez, the unexpected development was the surprisingly warm relationship that grew up between Harold Macmillan and John F. Kennedy.[12] There was then nothing very positive to note until Thatcher and Reagan, and thereafter another gap until Tony Blair and Bill Clinton.

Thatcher and Reagan, and Blair and Clinton, were linked by shared political vision or instincts, but even so the degree of influence was not constant. Reagan invaded Grenada without consultation and tried to impose extraterritorial sanctions on trade with the Soviet Union; Clinton was less than helpful on Northern Ireland on a number of occasions. With the present President Bush, there seems no basis for a general political alignment, but the British prime minister has sought to identify himself very closely with the United States, not least on and by the deployment and use of military force. On the eve of the first Blair-Bush meeting, the president's national security adviser said that it was part of the special relationship. However, increasing unilateralism in Washington in the wake of the 11 September attacks may imply a very restricted view of what such a relationship means from the U.S. end, notwithstanding the ability of the two leaders to get along together. Despite Mr. Blair's efforts, it is not clear that Britain has gained any leverage on American policy formation (that is, over what to do, rather than how to do it—where there may have been some impact). Increasing divergences in respective national views over Middle Eastern issues in particular may make it impossible for him to follow Mr. Bush quite so closely in the future, though there are few signs that the prime minister will seek to distance himself.

In short, despite some real substance, there has not been a continuous or consistent happy relationship between British and U.S. leaders since the Second World War. There was little special about the relationship in the immediate postwar years, except for the intelligence dimension, and it may be significant that the United Kingdom remained in some ways the senior partner up into the 1950s—in other words, the relationship remained special in an area where Britain had something that the United States needed. Beyond this specific area, there have been very tight bounds to the extent of British influence upon the United States and, in particular, to its impact on high-level policy formation.

CHAPTER THREE

The American Half Century,
and European Contrasts

The United States ended the Second World War as a global power. It largely framed the postwar economic system, played a very major role in the creation of the United Nations, and almost single-handedly set about remaking Japan. Within a few years it had started the reconstruction of Europe through Marshall aid, and from 1949 was bound into the military security of that area through the Atlantic Alliance, based on the Washington Treaty. Europe was perceived as the most important area of American interest, at least from 1949, although the Middle East and Asia were also major areas of U.S. involvement from about the same time. As British power declined in the former, the United States came to have an increasingly important role there, while the Korean War and Indochina brought it into involvement on the mainland of Asia.

Roosevelt had visions about managing the world in collaboration with the USSR. Truman came to a different view about that and quite speedily saw the need to confront Soviet ambitions. His views, so far as Europe was concerned, bore fruit from 1947, the date of the Marshall Plan and the Truman Doctrine. (Marshall's great speech, launching what was to become known as the plan, was specifically designed to win over the critics of the doctrine.) That year also saw the breakdown of discussions with the Soviet Union on the future of Germany. In the light of that, Ernest Bevin, Foreign Secretary, told Marshall that there would have to be an understanding (though not a formal alliance) between the principal Western countries to convince the USSR that it could advance no farther. By 1949 that thought, aided by the fall of Czechoslovakia and the Soviet attempt to cut off Berlin, had grown into the Washington Treaty, though even then both the drafting of its Article 5 and the explanations given to the U.S. Senate avoided, or rather sought to avoid, any automatic or long-term engagement of American forces in Europe.

For some forty years after 1949, the initiative, diplomatic as well as military, in European and other security regions, largely rested with the United States, which was now one of the two major world powers. In European security it played the pivotal role and was generally able to get its way on all significant issues. In particular, the structure and development of NATO reflected its wishes. It enjoyed, moreover, some political and diplomatic successes, notably over Berlin and German unification—in which last it had the decisive voice, playing a more honorable role than the European powers generally. Nevertheless, in the same period the United States fought an unsuccessful war in Indochina and saw significant policy reverses in the Middle East. Moreover, until the end of the Cold War, the United States was to a degree balanced militarily by the Soviet Union and was accordingly limited in the scope of its military and to some extent political and diplomatic interventions.

That changed with the collapse of the Soviet Union. At the beginning of the twenty-first century the United States had more political power than any other nation or group of nations, not least because of its military power—in which after 1991 no state could possibly rival it. The United States was supreme by almost any measure, in terms of defense budget and general high-performance military systems, force-projection capabilities, naval tonnage, numbers of advanced combat aircraft, nuclear submarines, and advanced surveillance and reconnaissance systems, including space assets. It retained, moreover, the leading global economic role, though other international actors also had significant economic influence and from time to time U.S. supremacy was felt to be under challenge from Japan or Europe.

Military, economic, and political power are intimately linked. Without economic power, military power will not last; without military power, economic power can be rapidly eroded. Political power usually reflects economic or military power or both. Most often, it principally reflects the latter and may in fact enhance it by providing allies, support, or acquiescence. Despite its apparent and real supremacy, from the beginning of the twenty-first century U.S. political power was, however, under challenge from outside actors, state and nonstate. Psychologically, the challenge culminated in the terrorist attacks of 11 September 2001, which demonstrated (inter alia) the defect of relying mainly on military instruments to make the United States secure but led nevertheless in due course to the national security strategy of September 2002. That document makes manifest that the United States intends to maintain military supremacy over all potential contenders and that it is more and more likely to try to operate outside the international system that others follow, however imperfectly.

U.S. Unilateralism

From the very beginning, even before independence, a strand of exceptionalism ran through a number of the communities that became the United States, a theme derived in part from English Protestantism. Today, American exceptionalism takes many forms.

It shows in rejection of attempts by others to do what the United States itself regularly does in terms of imposing its own conditions and laws; in a belief that the United States has the right to do what it wishes in almost all circumstances; and in a sense that American soil is sacred. The latter was a major factor in the drive for missile defense and in the rejection of intrusive verification arrangements in connection with chemical and biological weapons. (Logically, the exposure of the real vulnerability of the United States might have been expected to lessen the emphasis on these aspects of exceptionalism, but it seems rather to have reinforced it in many quarters.) In sum, there is a widespread feeling in the United States that the country is, and should be, privileged as a very special power, with uniquely good laws and practices. (A somewhat more sophisticated version of this proposition is that as the United States has unique capabilities it also has unique responsibilities for global order and stability, and so should be privileged above other nations in the same way that the policeman has certain powers that the civilian does not. The flaw here is that policemen are given specific powers by law and are accountable to both the courts and police authorities for their actions and the use or misuse of their powers, whereas the United States is neither so empowered nor accountable.)

Linked with the sense of exceptionalism there have always been isolationist tendencies in American public opinion, though these have not prevented deep engagement with foreign countries. Much more significant has been unilateralism, the tendency for the United States to seek to be unconstrained by any outside power or agent. George Washington urged his countrymen to steer clear of permanent alliances with any portion of the foreign world; Thomas Jefferson advised peace, commerce, and honest friendship with all nations, entangling alliances with none. That guidance has generally prevailed, with the major exceptions of the post–World War II alliances, most especially NATO and perhaps, following 11 September, of the so-called war on terror.

As regards entanglement, even in the case of NATO the U.S. freedom of action was but little constrained, partly because of American preeminence, economic and military, and partly because despite all the rhetoric of the NATO guarantee, Article 5 of the Washington Treaty, drafted to be acceptable to the Senate, commits the United States to no more than taking such action as it deems necessary in case of an attack. As regards peace and commerce, the United States has been a leading force in trying to impose sanctions on various states that have aroused its displeasure, and the war on terror has led to the adoption of the maxim "who is not with us is against us"—which hardly makes for honest friendship, given the genuine differences of opinion that can arise in tackling some very difficult policy issues that pursuit of that war encounters.

Beyond particular alliances and their constraints, the United States has shown a general reluctance to be bound by international law and, at any rate in recent years, at least as much hesitation over international organizations. Its failure to join the League of Nations, its persistent difficulties with the UN, its general belief that it can, if need be, act unilaterally without UN Security Council authority, and so on, are matters of record.[1] The same is true, particularly in recent years, of its attitude to international treaties. The Senate's failure to ratify the Comprehensive Test Ban Treaty; the watering down of the verification provisions of the chemical warfare convention; the wrecking of verification of the Biological and Toxic Weapons Convention; the withdrawal from the Anti-Ballistic Missile Treaty; the stepping back from the Kyoto environmental accords—all betoken an approach that rejects outside constraints. As early as 2000 there were signs of more of this to come, with pressure for the weaponization of space.

All this made and makes for a large difference between most European states and the United States on the appropriate contributions to security of international law and international organizations. Given that there are undesirable agents and trends in the wider world, the question is whether they should be tackled unilaterally or multilaterally and, in any case, whether one should rely primarily on military and technical means or on political and diplomatic. American and European answers to these questions have differed. There is little that the United States alone can do to check weapons of mass destruction (WMD) proliferation. Some initiatives, such as missile defense, seem to assume that such proliferation is unstoppable and that the United States has to cope with the world that it will certainly produce. Europeans are more likely to ask why states proliferate and whether it would not be better to address the root causes, which with few exceptions are genuine security concerns. They would, in any case, wish to make and uphold effective checks on proliferation by treaties with as good verification procedures as possible.[2] The United States has different views, entertaining grave doubts about binding itself by treaty and about allowing intrusive verification of itself.

Following the 11 September attacks the United States proclaimed itself as engaged in a war on terrorism. There is almost universal agreement among governments that terrorism must be opposed, though there are differences about what constitutes it. The United States now makes opposition to terrorism something like an article of faith. Long experience has given some European states more relevant expertise than the United States, whose intelligence agencies before 2001 had hardly focused on the sort of skills necessary for combating the threat and whose machinery of government had serious deficiencies with respect to it.[3] Europeans are much more likely to ask why terrorists are motivated to act as they do. Many in the United States could not see the connections between what the United States had done and not done and the attacks of September 2001; moreover, many there do not understand that there will be serious risks as long as there remain areas of grave deprivation, misery, and deep resentment at what is seen, whether accurately or not, as the perpetration of injustice, political or economic, by the powerful.[4]

In part, the differing approaches are a reflection of relative military strengths—the Europeans lack overwhelming military power and so must seek other ways to attain their ends. Matters go deeper than that, however. The very existence and functioning of the EU has amounted to training, of a sort that the United States has never experienced, in the sharing of sovereignty, even though this has only recently started to affect the classic concerns of diplomacy. The longer diplomatic tradition in at least some European countries is also relevant. For the nineteenth century, and almost all the first forty years of the twentieth, major European powers were themselves the world powers. Their successes and influence were not usually the result of overwhelmingly powerful military forces. In the earlier years, the Concert of Europe meant limiting each nation's own ambitions and actions; hegemony was not the name of the game, at any rate between 1815 and 1914. All this gives Europeans a different perspective on international relations and security tools, an outlook reinforced in many cases by consciousness of the direct impact of major wars on their societies and well-being.

Economic Power

The economic dominance of the United States became a major global factor after World War Two. Europe was devastated; most other parts of the world had not been economically developed. The United States had a booming economy and was the great creditor nation. Its industries were technologically advanced, and the rules and framework of the world economic system were largely set, through the Bretton Woods agreements, in terms advocated by the United States and that met U.S. requirements. That picture had been modified by the end of the twentieth century by the growth and recovery of Europe, the rise of Japan and certain other Asian economies, and by the hastening development of China and India. The latter two, the last in particular, still have far to go but the United States is no longer a unique economic actor.

In terms of workforce flexibility, technical and scientific base, and general entrepreneurial qualities, the U.S. economy has great strengths that may keep it in the top league throughout the twenty-first century. Underlying it are certain social weaknesses, notably the poor underclass and limited provision for it; however, there is movement out of the underclass, and for Americans not born into it perhaps more upward mobility is possible than in most other societies. The very fact that the United States is legally one country also brings advantages in certain matters in terms of economies of scale. By the end of the twenty-first century U.S. shares of industrial and global economic output will almost certainly be smaller than at the beginning; some industries and activities will have collapsed. However, the country as a whole is likely to stay near the forefront of developing technologies. It will still wield very substantial economic power, which will provide important inputs to military and political power.

An immediate result of the attacks of 11 September was the laying out of additional money, much of it for homeland defense (including pressing ahead with missile defense, which, whatever its theoretical virtues, is clearly not a counter to terrorist or similar assault on the continental United States) and the retention of military programs that might have limited utility but that in the present climate no Washington player wishes to be seen scrapping. That spending connects with the most significant foreseeable change in the American economic position, a change that concerns the dollar. The country runs very large and unsustainable fiscal and current-account deficits. The dollar has fallen and may well fall farther, with major impact on the ability of the United States to finance its lifestyle and consumption. That will have psychological effects at home and abroad, and so will affect its political power.

Military Power

The United States sees military force as a key investment and spends more than the EU, Russia, China, and Japan together on defense; this lead is set to increase. Moreover, most of the other technically advanced nations with military capabilities are its allies. Under the circumstances, it might have been a source of astonishment that the United States continues to spend as it does and to seek ever newer and more advanced systems.[5] However, it aims to acquire and maintain military superiority in any and all circumstances and to avoid the rise of any military rival.[6] It has continued to pull farther ahead in total expenditure and technical developments, and farther away in its views on the need for and utility of military force in international affairs. The forging ahead with such technical developments as network-centric warfare and such doctrinal issues as preemption or even the use of nuclear weapons for war fighting means that those who cannot or do not wish to wage war the American way need to consider both how and to what extent they can collaborate with the U.S. military and, to the extent that they do not do that, how they can protect and further their interests where military force is a necessary factor.

The United States cultivates a so-called warrior ethos within its armed forces; it has in the recent past espoused a doctrine of overwhelming force, arguing that when American troops are committed they should be in such numbers and wield such firepower that they can quickly overcome any opponent. That doctrine may have been modified by the experience of the 2003 war in Iraq and its aftermath, but it, and the associated but separate issue of seeking high-technology solutions to military problems, still influences the general approach to many security situations. Indeed, the emphasis on seeking overwhelming force through technical solutions seems likely to continue to be a major driver in the evolution of U.S. military capacity.

Before 2003, the United States had generally sought to reserve its military for the most testing, but at the same time least likely, cases of conflict, and it was most unwilling to risk its troops in many actual crises in ways that might have helped resolve them.[7] In the light of Vietnam and then Somalia, there was a general American reluctance to risk casualties, an effort to avoid them by technical solutions and combat at stand-off ranges, an unwillingness to use U.S. troops in situations that did not call for the top end of the spectrum of military activity. Some remnants of those attitudes are still to be found, but the terrorist attacks and the connection that the administration made, rightly or wrongly, between them and replacing the Iraqi regime have produced at least a short-term willingness to use the military for potentially hazardous missions. There is now certainly a readiness to incur at least moderate casualties when vital national interests are felt to be at stake. Still, it is too soon to judge whether that will last; the steady, though in total quite small, attrition in Iraq since victory was declared may have reopened some sensitivity on this score, though President Bush's reelection may argue in the other direction.

Linked with the emphasis on serious war fighting, and because of the stress placed on force protection, U.S. troops have not been wholly, or even very, effective at dealing with the complex security situations involving peacekeeping or nation building that have become of ever-increasing importance. The postconflict incidents in Iraq in which civilians were killed by U.S. soldiers unable to handle close contact and gendarmerie operations effectively show that there are situations and therefore security problems where American forces are less than effective.

By way of contrast, the use of European militaries in support of the civil power and in peacekeeping has given the countries concerned insight into the contributions that can be made in crisis management and maintenance of civil society. Nevertheless, many Europeans are too reluctant to see the need for force and too ready to abdicate demanding military options to the United States. Free from the risk of a serious war in Europe, they are generally too content not to develop the capabilities for significant military action. Granted, they do not need to match the level of technical development to which the United States aspires, since that is generally geared to long-range, high-intensity battle and the particular American concerns; nevertheless, Europeans do need to take defense more seriously and to invest more in certain vital capabilities. In particular, they are unable now to deploy, command, supply, or sustain well equipped and coherent forces away from their borders. Two individual states (Britain and France) can do that on a modest scale, but either would be hard pressed to deploy more than a division out of Europe or to wage a substantial air campaign with precision guided munitions. Partially in consequence of this weakness, Europe has much less influence politically (e.g., in the Middle East or Asia, or even in and over Cyprus) than is appropriate or might be expected given the facts of history, geography, and economics.

Some years ago a RAND study estimated that the Europeans spend about two-thirds of what the United States does on defense and get for their money only about one-tenth of the deployable forces. Since then there has been some movement toward greater effectiveness in European forces, but also cuts in defense budgets. Europeans now spend about 40 percent of what the United States does on defense. All in all, they have too many forces and platforms of the wrong sort, too little logistic capability, insufficient intelligence assets, and too few smart weapons. Little of that shortfall will be cured by progress toward the EU's "headline goal"—"to be able by 2010 to respond with rapid and decisive action applying a fully coherent approach to the whole spectrum of crisis-management operations covered by the Treaty on the European Union."[8] The problem is not numbers of infantry or even jet aircraft; it is the ability (political and practical) to deploy infantry and sustain it, of aircraft to find their targets and hit them in all conditions, and of Europeans to plan and direct campaigns. The United States will (rightly) not regard the Europeans as serious military players until they have made themselves much more effective.

Before the Iraqi crisis of 2003 all this threatened a de facto, but unacceptable, division of responsibilities across the Atlantic, with the Europeans alone engaging in local crisis management (which may be a frequent requirement) and incurring casualties thereby, but the United States either demanding leadership of the operation or else interfering politically, thus putting the Europeans at risk while frustrating their political objectives. In practice, the Europeans were reluctant to undertake alone even the tasks within their capabilities, mainly hoping to lock the United States into a common position. Meanwhile, by virtue of being the only state capable of significant power projection, the United States assumed control in other areas, including defending militarily common interests in the Middle East or Asia, conducting operations in accordance with its own approach.

So far from the post–11 September terrorist threat bringing about a change in U.S. views on the role and nature of military force or collaboration on intelligence and police issues that would make the Europeans more credible security partners, major new tension arose from the Americans' willingness to use force against the Iraqi regime at a much earlier stage than almost any other country wished. Nevertheless, to deal with current security threats the United States needs international cooperation on some aspects of military operations, for the use of bases or airspace, for local knowledge and skills, and quite possibly for the execution of certain things that the U.S. military does not do very well, as well as police, justice, and human intelligence. There is also, since the (at least nominal) handover of political authority to a new Iraqi government, a deeper appreciation in Washington of the political legitimacy that wider international support can bring.

Political Power

In some parts of the world U.S. conventional military strength remains an undoubted asset and a major source of political power. That is so in Southeast Asia, where it has an important stabilizing role between China, Japan, and Korea. Some of those states may feel a degree of resentment against what they may see as hegemonic pretensions, but on the whole military power readily equates with political influence there.

The same is true to an extent in the Middle East. There, however, matters are complicated for the United States by the rejection of modernity by some elements in Islam (the United States being in some respects the embodiment of modernity) and by its involvement with Israel. The connection of the 11 September attacks with both Islam and the Middle East demonstrates that there are limits to the leverage that military power brings. Indeed, the very superiority of U.S. arms and aspects of American culture foster a reaction that involves other security needs.

Political power in the developed world is in part a function of economics; in part it is also a matter of opinion. There are expectations—a habit of acquiescence, a memory of different times. All these give the United States some control over the policies and aspirations of European states, and of some others. There are great difficulties in envisaging how that form of power will develop in the coming century. On the one hand, globalization will spread aspects of American culture and influence deeply into every society. As more countries join the world economic order they will be influenced by the economic and financial policies of so important a player there. Some will see close links with a major military power as their safeguard against outside or internal instabilities. Others will continue to feel, even if for no demonstrable reason, that transatlantic links are essential to their security. Significant U.S. political power will therefore last well into the twenty-first century, perhaps right up to its end.

However, there are substantial questions about how that power will be used; about its weakening from the lack of an appropriate framework in which it can be deployed; and about how other power centers will develop, power centers that may work in harmony with the United States but that could, if not sensibly handled, become rivals.

U.S.-European Differences in Security Interests, Real and Perceived

Following the Cold War, the nature of security changed profoundly as regards both factors and actors. For the world as a whole, there will be major stresses from population growth, economic development, and environmental pollution. The latter two are linked, positively and negatively. Economic development is essential if political stresses of a most serious kind are to be contained. However, such development, if done along the lines of the twentieth century, will bring great environmental stresses. Different

routes will have to be sought. Of higher immediate profile are terrorism and the proliferation of weapons of mass destruction—two different problems but possibly linked,
and in American eyes certainly to be considered together. They were of different sa-
lience in different countries, both before and after the attacks of 11 September 2001.

The transatlantic differences on proliferation, terrorism, and the so-called states of
concern were not only of perception. Despite their having much in common, there are
differences in security interests between the United States and Europeans. These arise
largely from the U.S. concern and willingness to exercise power and influence, and its
having undertaken defense obligations, especially in Asia and the Middle East. The
United States is deeply engaged in the former, with preparations for major war fighting. European interests there, on the other hand, are largely economic. Korea, Taiwan,
and Japan are not hard security issues for most Europeans, except as regards North Korea, which is a common source of concern in view of its ballistic missile and nuclear
programs; they exercise the United States much more.

On the Middle East, including Iran and Iraq, the United States and the Europeans share
many interests, but both are deficient in one way or another in pursuing them. There
are strong currents in Iranian political life seeking to return to normal and proper international relations. Bringing that about must be a common objective, but many influential parties in the United States remain fixated on earlier injuries and apparently
fail to understand the pressure that must lead any Iranian government to consider the
acquisition of WMD and to seek a major regional role. The EU efforts to engage the
Iranians in the coalition against terrorism and to induce it to take a proper grip on its
nuclear program may mark the start of better things, but it must be admitted, more
than most European players do, that inducing the regime to modify its most objection-
able internal practices and genuinely to forego the option of nuclear weapons on a permanent basis will be very difficult. As regards Iraq, the Europeans failed to appreciate
the dangers from the regime; the U.S. administration failed to see how its own actions
would tend to frustrate its long-term objectives and provide drivers for terrorism.
More generally, it did not appreciate how its very successes and their impact were
provoking reactions against it, some merely of disgruntlement (China and India, Iran, and
many other states are most unlikely to welcome global efforts at permanent unilateralist
U.S. leadership), some of the sort that resulted in the 11 September incidents.

Also, with respect to the Middle East there has been a long-standing U.S. inability to see
that its interests are not identical with those of Israel. (Even in the Cold War that may not
have been the case; with its end, the divergence is manifest.) On the whole, the Europeans
are clearer sighted on the issues and Western interests but have only recently been able to
make any noticeable contribution to the resolution of the Palestinian problem; even now

what they can do and what they might do is still narrowly limited. Meanwhile this issue greatly complicates American efforts on proliferation and terrorism.

Until September 2001, the United States generally felt secure behind its ocean barriers from most threats, except ballistic missiles, but made much of the WMD threat and of "rogue states." Europe is geographically closer than the United States to most would-be proliferators, easier of access from countries from which migrants are likely to come, and it has suffered more terrorist attacks; still, it had not shown the same zeal for missile defense or pursuit of rogue states. The more profound differences stemmed from the fact that despite domestic parochialism and the pressure of sectional interests, the United States has a global view and major global responsibilities. Many European states failed and still fail to take such a view. Thus although the objective differences in long-term interests are relatively few, and mainly related to the pursuit of national advantages in trade and influence, European and U.S. security concerns frequently diverge.

The great difference in perceived security interests is between the European view of a world regulated by international law and involving a multilateral approach, and an American vision that, at the end of the day, believes that the ultimate safeguard of its interests is to be free to act without outside constraint, conducting military operations strictly in its own way, impeded as little as possible by alliance structures or the views of coalition partners. That in turn requires overriding military power and a willingness to prevent any challenger to that power from arising while developing high-tech warfare on a level and a scale that cannot be matched by others and that isolates the nation from potential partners in the conduct of much military business of its own.

The United States fails to see the need to consolidate a law-based approach to security problems or to build international institutions or support that might help safeguard its security. The launching of a war without UN sanction to effect regime change in Iraq only intensified the rejection of hegemonic tendencies. It badly damaged the Security Council; it demonstrated the decay within NATO; because of the divergence between Britain, France, and Germany it gravely set back EU efforts to make a Common Foreign and Security Policy (CFSP) and European Security and Defense Policy (ESDP). It produced major splits in Europe and between long-standing European NATO allies and the United States. Both Europeans and Americans now need to reflect hard on where they stand and, more particularly, whither they should go. In many ways, despite attempts to mend fences, the attack on Iraq may mark a more important watershed than its precursor, the 11 September incidents.

CHAPTER FOUR

The United States and Europe in the Twenty-first Century

Some perceptive judgments (such as those by Alexis de Tocqueville) in the nineteenth century notwithstanding, an assessment made in 1905 about the principal actors and factors in international relations and international security in the coming century would almost certainly have been significantly inaccurate. The United States might not have figured very prominently; Germany would probably have been seen as a major actor throughout; Asian powers (with the exception of Japan) would have probably not made much of an appearance. Coal and steel would have been high on the list of important factors; oil, gas, and the internal-combustion engine would have been there but probably not too significant. Likewise, aviation would have had a mention and perhaps chemical industries, but little would have been made of their potential applications in war, while nuclear energy and WMD as the twenty-first century perceives them would have been absent. The current and prospective uses of space and widespread and instant communications would have been unlikely to feature. Globalization, on the other hand, might have been seen as playing a larger role in the twentieth century than it in fact did, at any rate until toward the very end.

Some Factors in International Relations and International Security

Describing what one's forebears or predecessors failed to foresee can be an easy game but perhaps not a very useful one. The point in raising it here is to instill a sense of humility in projecting how the twenty-first century may evolve and what the factors and actors may be. The comments on politics and economics that follow do not seek to replicate deep scholarship on those subjects. Issues of democracy, markets, and free trade have a copious professional literature; the aim here is not to provide definitive answers but to raise an awareness that there are very big questions yet to be resolved. Thus in suggesting how Europe and the United States might collaborate or how the United Kingdom might sort out its role in the world, one needs to acknowledge that the answers are unlikely to be simple and that the course of development is likely to be very uncertain. Those are, of course, very good reasons for thinking hard about the issues and not simply assuming that oft-repeated formulae from the last sixty years hold all the truth.

So much has been written on the "revolution in military affairs" and then a successor concept, network-centric warfare, that one might be tempted to believe that the course of security in the twenty-first century has been well charted and that, aside from variations in detail and taking account of the possible use of terrorism at the strategic level and the use of WMD (acknowledged by both the United States and the EU as major security threats), the core structures of hard security can be known tolerably well. However, there is at least an implicit contradiction—if network-centric warfare may indeed be essential for all-arms, joint, twenty-first century battle, it is not clear what it has to do with countering strategic terrorism of the sort that involves suicide bombers, criminal networks, and widespread religious ferment. That is not to deny that network-centric warfare may be useful for such things, but if so, development will be called for beyond what has so far been put forward.

More fundamentally, it is not beyond doubt that there is a truly strategic threat from terrorism, in the sense that a major state's very being or way of life could be so subverted by terrorist actions as to remove its ability to safeguard the generality of its vital interests. The attacks of 11 September on the United States certainly dealt a heavy blow to American confidence and have had a major influence on the laying out of resources and the organization of security machinery, but with all respect and sympathy for the victims and their families, one has to question whether, as against deaths from other sources and economic losses from other causes, the United States was fundamentally damaged by the attacks. Middle Eastern societies have suffered far heavier attrition; the deaths in Northern Ireland, admittedly over some thirty years, were on a greater scale. What was changed by 11 September were American perceptions of security and risk. Those are important, but one must try to see the changes in the perspective of a hundred years and of other changes and potential happenings.

The devastation around the Indian Ocean caused by the earthquake and tidal waves in December 2004 showed what natural disasters can do, particularly to relatively poor societies. It is entirely possible that future disasters, attributable to global warming, will create equal devastation during the twenty-first century. There is widespread agreement that major changes associated with global warming are in train, but there is not yet a common psychological perception of the death and destruction that they may entail. As regards WMD, in contrast, there is an all too lurid sense of what could be involved. A successful nuclear attack on a city would indeed cause major destruction and loss of life. Such a thing must be avoided if at all possible. However, a single attack would not mean the end of civilization or life as most people know it. It might well not even be a devastating blow (in a strict sense) to the country (as opposed to the direct victims) suffering it. The life of the nation would in many cases resume within a relatively short period. The same is likely to be true, in many if not most cases, of a chemical or a biological attack. Chemicals can be extremely toxic; however, delivering sufficient doses to kill significant numbers of people is difficult and may require hundreds, even thousands, of tons of them. Biological attacks require much less weight of agent, but again, reliably delivering sufficient lethal doses to inflict widespread death is fairly difficult. An epidemic, once started, can go through an unprotected population swiftly, but with most agents at least some protective measures are possible. In short, an attack with WMD would not simply wipe out a victim country or society. There could be great damage or death, but that is most likely as a result of a nuclear attack, which requires an elaborate infrastructure, or of some forms of successful biological attack. There is no room for complacence, but it is necessary to view assessments of the nature of security threats to developed (Western) societies with somewhat more skepticism than is generally used. There are real threats, but they need to be viewed in a perspective different from that of the last security scare.

Other issues about which skepticism needs to be generated and facile assumptions swept away include the general benefits of democracy in all circumstances; the ability of markets to solve all economic problems (and some would say to solve social and political ones too); and the order of priorities in nation building and the establishment of functioning societies. All those are, of course, linked. The usual assumptions have much going for them—which is why they have become working assumptions in the first place. All however, need to be scrutinized as rigorously as any other hypothesis advanced as to how systems, human or mechanical, work.

Democracy is the great untouchable issue of the twenty-first century. It is assumed to be universally good and desirable and, with possible short transitional periods, universally applicable—to which there are several points to be made. Firstly, there is often widespread confusion as to whether is meant responsible government, the rule of law, or reasonable and liberal (in the Lockean sense) laws. The three are different and must have different priorities. Secondly, responsible democracy without the underpinning of political education, the spirit of yielding more or less gracefully to the results of the process, and effective mechanisms to give effect to selection by voters (ands so also to defining who votes) will not last. The experience of decolonization in Africa gives an awful warning—Westminster-style democracies in many cases simply turned within very few years into long-lasting dictatorships.

Markets are essential for long-term economic success. However, it is not sufficient simply to decree that there should be markets. Markets are defined by institutions; they
function in the light of information; and they have to have effective underpinning from
both criminal and civil law. Moreover, the existence and effective use of markets is not
the same as free trade. The latter is in the longer term essential for widespread prosperity, but defective markets and the need to cope with issues of unfair competition or
monopoly mean that some limitations and controls are sometimes necessary in the
shorter term.

Changing Security

The United States originally engaged in Europe for security reasons. From 1942 to
1992, that engagement was essential for the security and well-being of both itself and
Western Europe. Up to 1945 American forces, and supplies and materiel even more so,
were required to defeat a hegemonic power that had occupied much of the continent.
After 1945 the eastern part of the continent was occupied by another hostile and
heavily armed power that the Europeans, weakened by the Second World War, could
not resist on their own. U.S. leadership, military and political, was essential and almost
universally acceptable. Thus, the United States had an indispensable role in European
and global security beginning in World War II and extending throughout the Cold
War; even with the end of the latter, political and military factors gave it an active part
in Europe up to the end of the twentieth century.

Engagement in Europe, and political, economic, and military leadership served, of
course, U.S. interests, in addition to European ones, very well. It brought influence, if
not control, over European foreign and defense policies; it ensured that a Soviet Union
viewed as aggressive would not overrun the economically valuable and politically vital
lands of Western Europe or gain a major strategic base in the Near East or Mediterranean. Europe was truly America's first line of defense, unsurpassed in strategic importance and with shared views on many global issues. Despite the many and long-running
weaknesses in European defense expenditure and planning, and chronic disputes on
burden sharing, holding the Cold War line with the Europeans was cheaper for the
United States, and more effective, than attempting it without them.

With the end of the Cold War, the nature of security in general and of European security in particular altered, and that changed the calculations on both sides of the Atlantic. There is little outside threat of the classical sort to almost any country on the
continent. (Turkey, which lies almost entirely outside Europe and faces both internal
and external security problems, is a partial exception, as were the states of the former
Yugoslavia, which also had major internal problems and confronted threats from
among themselves.) Instead, new threats, or threats on a new scale, ranging from

criminal activity and terrorism to the proliferation of weapons of mass destruction and trafficking of various sorts, have become the main security concerns in Europe, as in many other places. There is also the impact of the spillover—the impact, direct or indirect, of ethnic and other civil conflict either in Europe or, now more likely, outside. Both in Europe and elsewhere there is a general need to stabilize countries with weak political systems, very limited resources, and inadequate management and administrative skills. In all of this, U.S. military power has proportionately less role to play than it did in confronting the Soviet Union.

The potential contributions of European countries to confronting these new problems may, in some respects, be relatively greater than their contributions to common security during the Cold War. Indeed, in some respects the Europeans, individually and collectively, contribute more in money, action, and engagement to the new security agenda than Americans. In some of the necessary security skills and aptitudes they are at least as well versed as the latter. However, their ability to contribute useful military forces (and it is to these rather than to the other instruments of diplomacy that the United States tends to attach prime importance) in the areas that have become of most concern to the United States—the direct security of the United States is now much less dependent on military engagement in Europe—has recently been much less than it was before 1991. Most European militaries cannot project forces any distance, and few can provide forces that can fight the sort of intensive all-arms and joint campaign that the United States has waged in Afghanistan and Iraq. In short, the Europeans need the United States much less than they used to, and the United States has much less need to secure Europe militarily than it believed it needed to do in the Cold War; thus the parties are less valuable to each other than they used to be. The benefits to both parties from the United States having been in Europe are much less, and thus the costs are seen as less acceptable than in time past.[1] Even before the 2003 Iraq conflict, a number of Western European states were, therefore, less inclined to accept automatic American leadership.

Given the profound transition that security has undergone with the end of the Cold War, transatlantic relationships that were originally, and for long after, primarily concerned with security should also, prima facie, change. However, most parties have been reluctant to review the transatlantic relationships. The Europeans have shown, in general, a reluctance to take the steps necessary to address their interests and many of their security concerns on their own, while the United States has its own reason for maintaining the status quo—to preserve its earlier preeminence. It would be a major setback for American diplomacy, in terms of loss of influence, if the United States were no longer engaged in European security.

The breakup of the former USSR, which was the trigger for the change in the nature of security, came about with surprisingly little upheaval or bloodshed, except in the Caucasus. (There is still trouble between Azerbaijan and Armenia, and in Georgia; Russia itself is faced with a continuing war against insurrection in Chechnya, which, despite substantial military commitment, remains unresolved.) Thus, despite the foreseeable new security challenges, there was after the Cold War a general expectation of a "peace dividend." Not unreasonably, military expenditure in most of Europe and in the United States dropped markedly in the decade after 1991. However, it rapidly became clear that military capabilities were still required. Immediately after the Cold War there was the U.S.-led conflict with Iraq; victory came speedily to the coalition through an unhindered, massive buildup of men and materiel and the application of advanced technology. That was followed by a decade of turbulence in the Balkans involving war fighting and heavily armed crisis management. Meanwhile, the United States once more pressed ahead with technological developments in the military sphere. It expressed concern over the spread of WMD; there were in Washington very strong currents in favor of some form of missile defense, which led in the first G. W. Bush administration to the abrogation of the ABM treaty and the commitment of very substantial resources to the development of such defenses.

Europeans, having originally believed that they could mediate the issues in the former Yugoslavia themselves, rapidly found themselves without sufficient collective military force, political power and cohesion, or—and perhaps even most importantly—self-confidence to act without the United States. The EU and its member states had to rely on American support in military activity in Bosnia in the first half of the 1990s and in Kosovo in 1999; in the latter case the United States conducted an air campaign of a sort that the Europeans could not have mounted. On the whole, however, after its experience in Somalia in 1993, the United States was most reluctant to engage in peacekeeping or similar operations in the Balkans or elsewhere (though it was certainly prepared to engage politically in the Balkans at an earlier stage).

The Attacks of 11 September

The whole (altered) picture of global, including European, security and most especially U.S. attitudes was given a great jolt by the terrorist attacks of 11 September 2001, followed a year later by the administration's seeming determination to topple the regime of Saddam Hussein in Iraq. The latter effort went through unilateralist and then somewhat more multilateralist phases. Both it and the so-called war on terror showed great and, after initial sympathy following September 11, increasing divergences across the Atlantic, divergencies that widened as the war on terror was connected to regime change in Iraq.

The 11 September attacks showed that there could be a strategic threat from terrorism, in the sense of blows against a nation's heartland or vital interests; they also gave a boost to certain tendencies in the United States that were already manifest. Those included concern about the proliferation of WMD and the perception of a need for ballistic missile defense; they also gave a push to homeland security and led to a substantial uplift in the already very great U.S. defense budget. The fruit born of that last is likely to change profoundly how the American military wage their campaigns and draw the United States even farther ahead of, and so apart from, the military capabilities of the rest of the world. The upshot will probably make the United States unable, even if it were willing, to share the actual conduct of major, high-intensity, military operations. (It is already extremely reluctant to share their direction, because of its unilateralist approach to almost all foreign policy issues). These developments are linked to a distinctive American approach to war, essentially one of decisive engagement through overwhelming power, shared by few Europeans, and to a determination to exercise hegemony and allow no rivals to emerge that could contest U.S. military, or in many instances political, primacy.

September 11 brought out transatlantic differences over both the use and role of military force, as well as over the scope and role of international law, even the very nature of international relations. Meanwhile, attempts by some in the administration to link the rooting out of terrorism with the serious but different issue of WMD showed a further marked divergence of perspective. The developing situation in Afghanistan following the rapid toppling of the Taliban regime in 2001 and the problems that followed the swift initial military victory in Iraq in 2003 demonstrated the vital need for nation building—that is, the wider policy objectives of eliminating instability, the roots of terrorism, and the soil in which it may flourish can be achieved only by social, political, and economic change. It is not enough to win a war; one must also win the peace, for that is why one goes to war (or should do). The use of military power is very seldom sufficient, though it may be necessary, to bring about the needed changes.

The Europeans have so far had a much greater consciousness of that, and the EU has in principle a much wider range of instruments than has the Pentagon to use in pursuit of such an end. However, it has lacked coherence in the making of overall policies and strategies, and it has been ineffective in appreciating the necessary contribution of military capabilities to its security ends. Thus the twenty-first century has not got off to a good start in U.S.-European cooperation or relations.

In early 2003, acute differences over crucial foreign policy issues arose not only across the Atlantic but also between leading European states, all of this against the background of the U.S. concerns over Iraq and its possible WMD programs and the consequent decision by the United States and the United Kingdom to resort to war. Those divisions both emphasized the leading role that national governments were determined to play over foreign affairs—with few concessions to international or supranational institutions—and also made less likely any European common foreign and security policy over either transatlantic relations or Middle Eastern security. The divisions were not even offset by a determination among the leading players to sort out their own differences so as to ensure at least coherence between the policies of the major European powers, even if the EU itself lacked one of its own.

On a more positive note, following the difficulties that came in the train of military victory in Iraq there were, by the time of the U.S. presidential elections of November 2004, some encouraging signs, if no firm indication, that an approach that sought as wide a measure of international support or legitimacy as possible still commanded some measure of agreement in the United States. The national vote was split fairly evenly; President Bush was reelected, but many observers saw a quite stark division in the country. Nonetheless, the very fact of reelection perhaps confirmed the strength of unilateralist feeling, and it was noticeable in the campaign that international involvement in matters of U.S. security was regarded as dangerous ground (no international permission chits to be sought before American interests were defended). What can reasonably be said is, firstly, that some commentators and actors accordingly see a need to get things on to a better footing, in the sense of each side of the Atlantic treating the other with appropriate respect and seriousness, and secondly, that others believe the Europeans are not worthy of serious consideration (some of the reasons for the latter view are explored below). The first group divide, very broadly, into those who believe that it may be possible to return to an earlier era of close though updated relations and those who, while seeing the virtues of such closeness as may be attainable, consider that the last fifty-five years or so were an exceptional period and that a more distant relationship would be neither bad nor inappropriate.[2]

EU Policy Making

The EU is a unique and still developing institution that combines supranational with intergovernmental aspects. Its nature brings great benefits and some important increments of strength but also entails certain major weaknesses. Among the problems that tend to lower its credibility in the eyes of many in Washington, and not only those who are instinctive unilateralists, is the difficulty with which it formulates coherent policies, especially on issues that go to the heart of diplomatic and military affairs. A major requirement is improvement of the EU decision-making machinery. In addition, most European governments are reluctant to spend adequately on defense, even for a limited but necessary set of capabilities, let alone the scale of the United States. That again, quite properly, lessens European credibility in American and other eyes.

Europe is not a unified state and cannot readily make policy like one, either in the (supranational) Commission or in the Council of Ministers (i.e., national ministers), including the European Council (heads of government). The EU lacks apparatus for harnessing together the Council and the Commission; both bodies, and how affairs are handled between them, need to be addressed. Until Europe has done that, it will not be able to defend its own interests effectively, much less act as a force in the wider world.[5] Even then there will remain great difficulties, because of the role that individual nations will continue to play in foreign policy. The making of foreign policy is divided not only between the Commission and the Council but even more crucially between the EU and its member states. They jealously guard their prerogatives over war and peace, and the CFSP covers only a small part, at best, of European foreign policy. Until the tension has been alleviated in this sphere, as it has been in the economic, the problem will remain.

A related difficulty is the very different perceptions among EU members of their interests and of legitimate means for their promotion. Member states need to consider whether action by the EU, by members individually, or by a small leading group would best address and promote their interests in the world as it is. Most of them also need to consider whether their interests can be effectively promoted so long as they depend to the extent they do on another, non-European, actor whose interests are different, though having important elements in common. Of course, even if EU members were content to be dependent free riders, that might not be acceptable in the long term to the United States.

It is widely recognized that organizational and constitutional changes are required in the EU, but there has been great difficulty in reaching agreement across the Union about what should be done. The changes proposed in the constitutional treaty agreed at the Brussels EU summit of 18 June 2004 may help improve matters, though it is far from certain that they will ever come into force. In the security area the treaty proposes some modest reforms on decision making and the creation of a sort of minister for foreign affairs by merging the posts of the (ministerial) Council's High Representative and of the Commissioner for External Relations. This should, indeed, make for more coherence between Council (which will remain in the lead on foreign affairs) and Commission. There is also a very modest extension of the possibility of proceeding by majority vote rather than unanimity.

As regards defense, the treaty will make it easier for a group of member states to work together on military matters. In justice and home affairs, including police and judicial cooperation, there will be majority voting. This should facilitate the fight against crime and terrorism, although there are rather tight limits on what can be done. In short, some steps, if the treaty is implemented, will be made toward remedying the major deficiencies, but there will still be a long way to go before the European Union is a coherent security player.

The enlargement of the EU will in any case make coherent and speedy European decision making, and the whole complex set of relations between EU institutions and members, even more difficult unless there is radical reform of institutions and procedures.[4] There is as yet little sign of willingness to focus on the difficult issues involved, which are divisive not only between older and newer members but between large and small. Enlargement has brought in a number of new members from Eastern and Central Europe, mainly small, all poor, and most with particular inclinations to favor American policies, in part because of the American role in confronting the Soviet Union, and in part because of a concern about what the countries involved might see as the overweening influence of the major European states. Donald Rumsfeld, the secretary of defense, sought in 2003 to exploit this by pointing to these new members as the "new Europe" and seeking thereby to widen the fissures in the EU. More generally, such actions and statements raise the question of whether the United States is now concerned to divide and in that way more strongly influence European foreign and defense policy, rather than, as for many years past, foster greater European integration. In consequence, the EU may find it even more difficult than in the past to pursue effective policies distinct from those of the United States, or at any rate from those that the United States would wish Europe to pursue.

The essential question for the EU is: What is necessary to promote and protect, firstly, its members' own direct interests, and secondly, wider interests, so as to take its part as a rich group in promoting the general good? That extends to general policy issues as well as to the ESDP. There is agreement that some kind of military capability is required, but it has proved far more difficult to say of what kind or how much. It will be a long time before there is unanimity on such matters. The way forward for Europe will have to be collaboration in the first instance between the major diplomatic and military players, and with those smaller states that can and will act seriously in these affairs—in short a Directoire. Such language is, of course, *non communautaire*, but it was how much of the development of the Union itself was undertaken, by the Franco-German couple. (That axis cannot now be the motor for development of foreign and defense policies, though both countries must be involved.)[5]

Military Capability

At least as significant as the institutional problems and the ability of member states to block action is the lack of European will to use force in many (and for some states almost any) circumstances. While military force is less important than the United States believes, and development and creating appropriate international institutions are much more important in many circumstances, Europe needs to do much more, not least because until it does it will not be taken seriously by the United States or by many other actors. Whether Europe can rise to the occasion remains doubtful. Military assets and capabilities are tools for the pursuit of other policy objectives; they are not ends in themselves. Until the Europeans are clearer on general policy formulation, they will not become clearer on what they need for the military option and when and how to exercise it. Even when the general perspective becomes clearer, there will remain specific difficulties.

Effective military capability has three components: *will*, the willingness to use the military option, to kill and be killed; *policy*, in the sense of formulating an objective that can be effectively pursued and the ways in which that can be done; and *assets*—materiel, trained personnel, logistics, etc. Europeans have nothing like a common will in the sense above; they have great difficulty in formulating policy; and almost all are seriously deficient, and will remain so for many years, in the assets required for all but the smaller and simpler military operations. Willingness to be serious about military improvements as opposed to rhetoric about them is all too often lacking.

It was the realization that the Europeans lacked sufficient military power, self-confidence, and political coherence to act without the United States, coupled with concern that in Kosovo the Americans were unwilling to act, that led to the British-French St. Malo initiative in December 1998. This call for the development of European autonomous military capabilities might have been expected from France; at St. Malo, however, the initiative apparently lay with the British prime minister, who by this action reversed a very long-standing British position that European military developments must be within a NATO framework and wholly acceptable to the United States. He was able to do that despite, or perhaps rather because of, his closeness to the U.S. president, both personally and politically.

The initiative was taken up in and followed through by, at any rate in words, a series of EU (and NATO) summits—Vienna, Washington (NATO), Cologne, Helsinki, Nice (December 2000). Nevertheless, by 2001 the words remained generally more prominent than the augmentation of European military capabilities; most defense budgets were still showing no substantive improvement, although at its summit at Laeken in December 2001 the Union declared itself able to take on some crisis-management operations.[6] This progress and that made on the ESDP and toward the 2010 headline goal constitute a useful first step; however, it starts to establish neither the role that military capabilities should play in European security, nor the extent to which Europeans need to provide them, nor how they will devise comprehensive policies integrating their employment with other actions. Moreover, it is fitful and likely to stall.

Against that background, a division of labor between the Americans and the Europeans in which the former undertakes the serious military tasks and the latter the "soft security" (i.e., policing, gendarmerie, economic, political and legal development) options might superficially appear attractive. It might, in any case, come about de facto. However, it would be bad for the United States, because of the odium that military engagement can create and because of the ill effects of a one-sided approach to security. The world needs the effective engagement of the United States, and the United States needs to be able to ameliorate crises using many forms of engagement, applying military force only in those limited circumstances where it is necessary. Such a division of labor would be bad for the Europeans as well, because military action, when required, may set the terms on which nation building or other complex and long-running actions will be carried out. That is, in effect, the United States would dictate the policies, and the Europeans would have to cope with the consequences. That would tend to produce less than optimal effects in terms of overall security; it would also reinforce hegemonic and unilateralist tendencies in the United States. Above all, it is reasonable neither to expect the United States to bear all the burden of military engagement nor for it to solve problems that are of little concern to it. If military force is needed in some circumstances Europeans must look to play their part; otherwise all parties will feel the tension between desires, influence, and equitable burden sharing.

Future Transatlantic Relations

The transatlantic differences in political and military power more than ten years after the end of the Cold War were in some ways surprising.[7] The United States and the EU were comparable in economic size, with the EU having a somewhat larger population;[8] they had similar technological bases, and essentially similar levels of development. Together they produced some 58 percent of global GDP and accounted for more than 40 percent of international trade in goods and services. However, the United States had the advantage of a more truly unified market and economy; of substantially larger spending on defense (but also significantly greater security commitments, for example in Asia); and above all, for all the interagency friction and the checks and balances between different branches of government, of much more coherent policy-making structures. In short, the United States was a state where the EU was a new sort of political entity, going beyond nation-states but also comprising them.

In considering unilateralism and the willingness to use military power, it may be no coincidence that the United States has been for some fifty years the main home of international relations theory. Even if the direct impact of that on day-to-day policy formation has been relatively slight, the cumulative effect of tomes on realism, with its emphasis on force and hegemony, must have had an impact on the climate in which policy is formed, especially given the close links in the country between academia and the higher reaches of policy making.

At a more popular level, Hollywood, with its battle spectaculars and bad history, may also have played a role. The expectations among Americans of war and their understandings of their nation's past, present, and future influence are both probably shaped by films in a way in which European views are not. Linked with that is the continuous reinforcement of various American national myths. All nations have them, but those of the United States have been particularly important in creating a sense of solidarity in a nation of immigrants from increasingly diverse backgrounds. These myths tend to reinforce the transatlantic divide, to the extent that it comes from the American sense of exceptionalism, that America is in some sense a chosen society that could be to other nations as a beacon or a shining city set on a hill. Indeed, that sense of exceptionalism itself both stemmed from and, toward the end of the twentieth century, contributed to a sense of evangelical (in several senses) Protestantism that contrasted across a spectrum of political and religious attitudes with the more secular European outlook.[8] Indeed, in the United States there is not only a political spirit that springs from evangelical origins but also a genuinely religious Right, moved by religion itself. This affects U.S. foreign policies in several ways, not least as regards the Middle East.

Developments in the United States since 11 September, culminating in President Bush's reelection, have given a further stimulus to longstanding American unilateralist tendencies that will complicate all the transatlantic relationships. Even before that the Bush administration had made clear its reservations about, if not actual distaste for, limitations on U.S. freedom of action and sovereignty by international agreements. After the attacks, there was a period of restraint and some considerable efforts at seeking international consensus in the struggle against terrorism, but these became very attenuated as the months passed. The September 2002 *National Security Strategy of the United States* spelled out, if using carefully nuanced language, a strongly unilateralist and exceptionalist set of policies.

Even immediately following the attacks, when for the first time in its history NATO invoked Article 5 of the Washington Treaty, its mutual defense commitment, the United States preferred to deal with its allies bilaterally rather than through the alliance. As regards the actual conduct of operations in Afghanistan, it is understandable that the United States did not use alliance machinery; however, that it did not use NATO as a forum for consultation over what it saw (and sees) as the principal security issue confronting itself and others, and the one through which it appears or purports to view most international affairs, raised major questions about the role of the alliance.

The United States certainly seeks European support, but it would prefer that it not emerge as a result of the Europeans' cohering together. In the past, NATO provided an effective instrument for influencing European policies. The United States no longer feels that it will so function and appears to prefer to emphasize bilateral ties and to plan and conduct military operations through its own structures rather than alliance mechanisms. NATO itself suffered acute trauma in early 2003 from France and Germany's refusal to allow preparations to defend Turkey from Iraqi attack.

Leaders and Followers, Partners and Rivals

In transatlantic relations, the hard question is why 380 million (or more) tolerably rich Europeans should follow the policies of 276 million rich Americans—policies that are designed to meet the needs and aspirations of the latter—and why either party should think that it is right for the Americans to play a major role in providing for the security and well-being of the rather greater number of Europeans, and that according to an American prescription.[10] Clearly, given the congruence of interests in a liberal international order, both sides of the Atlantic have an interest in a very wide measure of working together, if that can be achieved. Both would benefit from acting together rather than pursuing separate courses, and it is almost certainly the case that the 5,500,000,000 other inhabitants of the planet would be better off if the Americans and Europeans acted together—the very poorest need all the help they can get from the engagement of the rich—but the issues are who would settle the action to be taken, and how, and who would pay.

In principle, relations between Europe and the United States should evolve toward the former's acquiring a role and influence, political and military, more commensurate with its population and wealth.[11] It would then be able to bear a fairer share of responsibility for global and regional security in the widest sense. The EU's endeavors to develop the CSFP and the ESDP, as well as the introduction of the common currency, should lead in that direction to the extent insofar as they are successful. However, for reasons related to the structural problems in the EU, grave divisions among member nations (especially after the 2003 war on Iraq), and at least to a degree, U.S. reluctance, neither of those policies is prospering strongly. Paradoxically, the increasing unilateralism of the United States may tend to produce European movement in the right direction—that is, toward the EU's being able to bear a fairer share of the security burdens. America will find it increasingly difficult to exercise leadership if it can attract no followers; the Europeans may conclude that they will have to be able to act themselves if certain things that they wish to see are to be accomplished. However, there will be significant problems in such evolution.

A whole range of issues from global poverty, through international development, to global warming can be tackled successfully only if the West as a whole, and that means mainly the United States and the EU, acts together. (Involvement by Japan, Canada, Australia, etc., is desirable and useful, but if the two major actors are not effectively engaged most actions of others will be in vain.) The EU and the United States should work together where they have common interests and where joint action would give greater leverage than unilateral interventions. These interests would include making democratic change and the consolidation of a law-based society in Russia irreversible. It should also cover international economic and trade relations and institutions; both the United States and the European Union have real interests in their smooth and free functioning and in the liberalization of trade; and both have lamentable protectionist tendencies and in particular an inability to deliver on reforms that would most help alleviate poverty and speed development in the poorer countries.

In principle, too, there is joint thinking to be done on the security issues of the Middle East, on whose oil both are dependent to a significant degree, and where perhaps the greatest challenges to Western security will have their origin. However, European military weakness will make the EU an unsatisfactory partner in that connection for some time. (U.S. shortcomings make it an unsatisfactory partner there in other ways, but for the Middle East military capacity is an indispensable part of any coherent security policy.) Nevertheless, they should address together the Israel-Palestine dispute. There the complicating factor is not European military weakness but, paradoxically, U.S. political weakness—American inability to master Israeli intransigence against any interference in how Washington misconducts its affairs and almost any outside involvement except that of the United States, which in many ways acts as an Israeli client state. This dispute is a major destabilizing factor in the area, one that needs to be addressed for its own sake as well as for reasons of regional development (economic, social, and political) and of mitigating a potentially widespread rejection of the West and its values. All in all, the Middle East is an area where Europe and the United States need to collaborate but that is at present a major apple of discord between them. They need to do better, with Europe making itself to be more effective and able as a partner and the United States believing less in its own monocular vision.

A historical survey of the twentieth century shows the Americans as having done much good for the Europeans, though less than the former commonly think.[12] For some fifty years, U.S. involvement was essential to the preservation of a liberal order in Europe. However, the very success of that engagement encouraged a dependence culture in Europe; Europeans forgot in many cases that they might have interests different, or at least separate, from those of the United States. Among at least some American policy makers there is a strong tendency to believe that what is good for the United States is good for the world as a whole; among others there has arisen the even more unfortunate belief that the United States can generally get what it wants on any issue because of its strength, and that the ability to get its way is sufficient justification for pursuing its own ends.

Although the genesis of the modern transatlantic relationship was in war and then in the security field, there has, since the time of the Marshall Plan in the late 1940s, always been a good deal of cooperation, bilateral and multilateral, going well beyond defense. It covers a wide range of economic and trade matters, even though disputes on steel, bananas, and development and debt can obscure the collaboration that takes place in the World Trade Organization (WTO), International Monetary Fund (IMF), and other international economic institutions. So far as security is concerned, the nature of the cooperation has changed, and that affects the relationship. New concerns call for cooperation of different sorts, most often not military, and in different ways—for example, to tackle terrorism or trafficking. Already, it has included wider issues as in the Organization for Security Cooperation in Europe (OSCE), and the NATO-Russia Council, as well as work among the Western permanent members of the UN Security Council. That said, even before the strains produced by the 2003 Iraqi war, there was a great deal of room for improving and extending the areas of transatlantic cooperation. Nothing since has changed the need for that, though the options may well have narrowed. There would be great benefit to be gained from a common approach to improving international security by strengthening the role of international institutions and of the rule of international law, but that is likely to bring on the first great difference with the United States.

As regards formal links between the EU and the United States, cooperation is based on the Transatlantic Declaration of 1990 and the New Transatlantic Agenda (NTA) adopted in 1995. There are summit meetings, working groups, and meetings of experts. Much of the dialogue is on trade, but the agenda is broadening. The NTA contains four broad objectives for U.S.-EU collaboration:

- Promoting peace and stability, democracy, and development around the world

- Responding to global challenges, including international crime and narcotics, and disease

- Contributing to the expansion of world trade and closer economic relations—the NTA calls for support for the World Trade Organization and strengthening the multilateral trade system

- Building bridges across the Atlantic by expanding commercial, cultural, educational, and scientific exchanges to enhance public understanding of the transatlantic relationship.

All those are highly desirable and make a sensible set of objectives; if zealously implemented they would make a significant impact on world affairs. However, what actually happens shows that reality is somewhat behind the ambitious words—the close institutional cooperation for which the NTA calls is not to be seen.

There are many reasons for that. Both the United States and major members states of the European Union often prefer to deal bilaterally. Part of the reason, though only part, is the clumsy machinery for representing the EU; another part is the Union's problem in forming coherent policies; a further significant factor is the safeguarding of national autonomy. Meanwhile, in Washington there are some issues surprisingly parallel to the problems of EU policy formation—the frictions in the interagency process and, especially since 2003, the desire in some parts of the U.S. machine to split Europe rather than collaborate with it.

Defining its own ends is a messier business for the United States than it is for most states. Firstly, there is the structure of the machinery of government, giving authority to Congress to block policies of the elected executive and also to strike out with policies of its own that may contradict the administration's. Largely because of the role and power of Congress, the decision-taking process is particularly open to manipulation by pressure groups, which may exercise influence quite disproportionate to their true significance in national life. The result can be policies that do not reflect the overall interests of the United States. Secondly, the Washington interagency problem is notorious; sometimes the United States is unable to speak with one voice unless the highest levels have been brought together. Such factors and the increasingly unilateralist U.S. approach to international affairs mean that no improvements in the consultative machinery with the EU will improve affairs much; a resolute determination to do better will be more important than the mechanical aspects of cooperation. Meanwhile, the fundamental issues that lie at the heart of transatlantic relations remain American unilateralism, whether based on its exceptionalist view of itself or on naked self-interest, and European strategic diffidence.

As justification for unilateralism, there is an influential view in Washington that there are many complex threats to the well-being and prosperity of the Western world and way of life and that only American power and coherence can protect the open, liberal order. In short, the United States may be a hegemon, but it is a benign hegemon, and living under its direction and influence is better than any realistic alternative for the world, particularly given European weakness, incoherence, and lack of global view. A complementary rather than contrary view is that U.S. interests require the possession of unchallengeable military power and the exercise of hegemony. The unique heritage of the United States is in this view a model for mankind, and therefore the nation must find no external impediment to doing what is necessary to secure its interests.

However, the United States is not uniquely wise. Even if it acts for and from the best of motives, the results may not be optimal; at the very least, reaction against American power may be traumatic. Acquiescence in U.S. hegemony might, in any case, prevent a better system from coming into being, by obstructing the development of international law and a more soundly based international system. Often the best may be the enemy of the good; here, perhaps, even if the benefits of present hegemony be accepted, the reasonable and present good could be the enemy of the better, the more enduring, and in the long run, the absolutely essential.[13]

Moreover, there are obvious dangers in the existence of any one overweening actor. There are, indeed, checks and balances within the United States but not between that country and the rest of the world. Its internal checks will not guide it to act in the interests of others; indeed, such is the nature of democracy and the American political system that they may well produce the precisely opposite effect. There is a great fund of goodwill in America, willing to do the right thing and to put problems right. However, for reasons having to do with how American politics works, that goodwill shows through in government action only sporadically and patchily. Meanwhile, there is in general no voice of a weight corresponding to the internal interests to argue with the administration on behalf of outside interests for different courses and different ways of doing things. That is good neither for global governance nor, in the long run, for the United States itself. There is no warrant for all other states, with their own distinct interests, simply to subordinate their judgment to that of a governmental machine that is all too fallible and often not prepared to work in good faith through international institutions. The United States will, very naturally, seek its own perceived advantages— that is, advantages as perceived by effective domestic interest groups. The results may provide common benefits, but they are at least as likely not to. Obvious examples are policies on the environment and agriculture.

In some areas, of course, any power has to be multilateralist except in the short term. On trade and economic relations, the United States is not supreme. Despite the leading role of the dollar, Europeans are much more its equals in the economic sphere than in the security one, and they are therefore often able to resist U.S. pressure there. Washington can impose tariffs unilaterally, but not on a long-term basis—at any rate, not without weakening the liberal order from which it benefits so much. In cooperation against crime and terrorism the United States needs the willing sharing of intelligence and information by others. In other longer-term security issues the EU, incoherent as it can sometimes be, is already playing a worthwhile role. The pressure at the end of 2004 to enforce a proper democratic outcome to the Ukrainian elections is one example;[14] another, where the United States has failed miserably and looks set to continue to do so for some time, is global warming and the limitations of greenhouse-gas emissions.

European leadership led to the Kyoto Treaty; unsatisfactory as that is, it is a good deal better than denying the problem and doing nothing. If this major problem is to be tackled it will be from the eastern side of the Atlantic, not the western.

On matters of security more narrowly defined, it is not clear that the United States is very open to outside influences. In that it is not, of course, unique. Issues of war and peace are notoriously matters for sovereign states, and that remains true of EU members, even though they have progressed beyond where the United States is in matters outside of the military security area. European soft power, or ability to influence others, is in itself inadequate to tackle many problems. Hard power remains necessary, and most of that can come only from the United States in the immediate future; the question is how will it be used, in conjunction with what soft power, within what framework, and to what ends.

A Summing Up

By wealth, population, technical base, and military power, the United States is rightly a major actor on the world stage and will almost certainly continue to be so for decades to come. Economically it has been so throughout the twentieth century; politically it has been so since 1941. All this once attached great importance to the different sets of transatlantic relations: those between the EU and the U.S. administration; those between the European members of NATO, individually and occasionally collectively, and the United States; and those that each major European country has—for instance, with the Department of State or Defense. The relationships were, and are, manifold, differing greatly in their intensity and impact; even Britain's much mentioned special relationship consists of at least three separate components.

Despite Paul Kennedy's warning in *The Rise and Fall of the Great Powers* (1988), there is no sign yet that the United States is exhausting itself. One day, however, its relative and possibly its absolute power may change. The Western European powers exhausted themselves in two world wars, which tended rather to enrich the United States and certainly resulted in the transfer of predominance to it. Few statesmen or diplomats could have foreseen in 1902 or even 1932 how completely French and British power would collapse; few foresaw in 1982 that within a decade the Soviet Union would be no more and that Russia would be a weak, impoverished power with an economy the size of (at best) that of a small Western European state. It would be against all historical experience for the United States to continue indefinitely to be so predominant as it was in 1945 or even as it is now. Nor is even its indefinite continuance as a major player guaranteed.

The European nations have been described as "postmodern";[15] that is, they have abandoned much of the classic insistence on sovereignty and a conflictual approach to the conduct of international relations. Despite the differences referred to above, that is true of the EU members as they stood before the 2004 enlargement. The United States, on the other hand, for all its modernity, in some ways remains a classic nineteenth-century actor, like Russia, China, or India. That involves severe limitations, in practice often greater than for any of those three states, on the role of international law and international institutions in the pursuit of U.S. interests. Unlike those other powers, however, the United States has overwhelming military, economic, and thence political power. It emphasizes sovereignty—its own, the absence of any authority that can bind the state or people of the United States unless they have most specifically consented to the binding, its general unwillingness to accept any outside rules, and its desire to interpret any rules it does accept in its own way.

America has never resolved its tension over the nature of its involvement with the wider world, which is, put simply, between diplomatic isolationism and engagement. It is not isolationist in the original sense of that term, nor has it been since the end of the nineteenth century. Its wider roles in Asia and the Middle East continue and arguably have increased with the ambitions of some in Washington to remake the latter in democratic form. Moreover, from 1945, despite considerable doubts in some parts of the American body politic about international law and engagement with international bodies, it has and exercises an influential role in global organizations, such as the UN, the WTO, the IMF, and the World Bank. However, its unilateralist tendencies draw on a heritage of seeking to avoid entanglement with others and their interests in any sense in which that would impede its own sovereignty, as well as on the feelings of superiority to other actors and all external authority. That same sense of superiority also, of course, drives many of the impulses toward engagement: the United States knows best, it has political and economic policies that are good for all, and it will seek to enforce them both in its own interest and more generally.

American military strength, while increasing in both relative and absolute terms, is likely to become less and less usable and useful, or rather, the problems that it can itself resolve will become a smaller part of the total. The marginal utility of additional carrier task groups or army divisions, above a relatively small number, will diminish rapidly, for the United States is already so much stronger in such things than any conceivable conventional enemy. As 11 September showed, asymmetric attacks are much more likely than conventional warfare. No state capable of balanced judgment is likely to wish to launch its aircraft against the U.S. Air Force; no naval combatant will seek oceanic conflict with the U.S. Navy. Both state and nonstate actors may, however, seek to make covert attacks on American civilian and military installations or to instill fear and disorder into American economic and social life. If a country can be identified as having been a base for the launching of attacks, military power enables the United

States to retaliate; indeed, the current administration has adopted a radical policy of preemption, ahead of the fact. However, if no such target can be identified, strong conventional armed forces may not be able to do very much to ensure security.[16] Military power of the sort that the United States now deploys with such superiority will not become redundant, a lesson that the Europeans in general have yet to learn; it will, however, yield markedly diminishing returns.

The United States enjoys not only great military power but also great soft power. That power is increased by checking unilateralist tendencies; it has been persuasively argued that America may weaken itself by seeking to go it alone and that there are real dangers for it in a foreign policy that combines unilateralism, arrogance, and parochialism.[17] The soft power wielded by the United States includes its language, which has become a lingua franca; the attractiveness of its popular culture, including music, dress, and fast food; its material success; and above all its role in globalization, including in communications and information technology. All of these may, of course, as well as providing major poles of attraction, produce a sort of Hegelian reaction or antithesis, fueling resentment in other civilizations and political systems.

The attractiveness of some aspects of American soft power is easy to see. Wealth, lifestyle, and freedom of expression all have a natural appeal to most, if not to all. Less easy to discern is why food, drink, and clothes in the American style should appeal so much, particularly to the young. Worldwide marketing is no doubt part of the answer; the halo effect of success—wealthy and prosperous people drink X, eat Y, wear Z; if I do likewise I too shall partake of their lifestyle.

However, the U.S. lead in globalization is, by definition, bound to diminish, at least in relative terms, as other parts of the world are linked up, acquire their own linkages, and participate in its further spread. The U.S. proportion of world population will diminish, while the absolute and relative wealth of India and China will almost certainly increase, and the same may be true of other populous countries. Technology and material wealth may still give an importance to the United States well beyond its population size, and in particular, military technology will give it great power in some spheres. However, in a globalizing world, where democracy and transparency will increase if the general American thrust succeeds, the United States will find it increasingly difficult to decline to share its wealth and prosperity, and certainly to share its hegemony.

The effect on the American outlook, on American exceptionalism, of more of the world either becoming more like the United States or reacting against it and its influence, is difficult to gauge. It may lead to a retreat into isolationism; it may enhance the unilateralist tendencies; it may even lead to a deeper engagement with the world and a greater degree of accommodation to differing views and interests. Whichever of these, or whatever combination of them, may be the result, there is little reason to believe that the European experience will be such that exactly the same policies and responses will be appropriate. Therefore, if the Europeans are to safeguard their interests, they will have to consider for themselves what those interests are and how they should be pursued. That is reinforced by the thought that adverse reactions to American actions may be reflected onto the Europeans as fellow capitalists and would-be neo-imperialists. That again is a reason for Europeans to seek their own policies and responses.

Given a free and prosperous Europe and a level playing field, it is not difficult to see that it too could enjoy significant soft power. The English language, or its absence, may be a partial barrier to some European cultural artifacts, but aspects of European style do have a high degree of attraction, not least in the United States. One reason Europe may not be able to compete is that, as the Victorians knew, trade follows the flag (as, of course, does in due course a reaction against the colonizers). Because the United States is heavily engaged in Korea, Taiwan, and Japan in a way that the Europeans are not, American culture has an easier entrée to parts of Asia. More global engagement by the Europeans would help a virtuous circle; more hard power would bring more soft power, though it might also provoke American resentment and resistance, unless matters were under U.S. control.

Both sides of the Atlantic should recognize that their common concerns now are very different from those of 1950. In the big picture, Europe should need the United States only in the same way as the United States needs Europe, in tackling global issues where multilateral cooperation represents the only way forward. However, in some important aspects the United States provides at present what Europe still lacks, relative coherence in foreign policy making (even when the policies themselves are open to question) and effective military force. Europe should set about remedying those lacks now. It should do so in a pattern that meets its needs, not necessarily American designs. Though that may not accord with immediate U.S. wishes it would be in the longer-term American interests, as well as those of Europe and the wider world. The United States and Europe as partners are more likely to be able to avoid the reaction against the U.S. way of doing things that will flow from its sole hegemony. Jointly, they may provoke a reaction against a perceived dyarchy, but that is less likely than a reaction against the United States alone. Meanwhile, there will be occasions when European interests as distinct from American ones will be safeguarded by the limitation of U.S. hegemony.

As for policy making, the Europeans have to address a unique problem, combining the institutions of the EU, and the result with that of the roles of the member states. Divisions between members large and small, new and old, will complicate matters. The larger European states will often be unwilling to yield substantial sovereignty to supranational machinery or to each other. The smaller will be jealous of any Directoire. Until effective compromises have been worked out the European Union will not be an effective diplomatic and security actor, and so transatlantic relationships will remain unbalanced and unsatisfactory.

As regards military matters, part of the solution is simpler than those for the political ones—that is, spending rather more, and spending much more effectively. The latter is technically easy, though politically difficult. The former will be difficult for some important players, like Germany and Italy. However, in principle, the military aspect is doable. The aim is not to create a second military on the American model but to provide an effective instrument to protect and pursue European interests, at first in Europe's backyard and then farther afield, be it in Africa, the Middle East, or wherever those interests may lie. Cooperation with the U.S. military is in principle highly desirable, but that depends in equal measure on whether the Americans desire and accept it, and make the necessary adjustments in their own policies and doctrines. All that is not very likely in the near future.

If the Europeans fail to sort out their political and military capabilities, the transatlantic relationships will indeed be made anew, but in a way in which Europe will have less influence on U.S. policies, not more. That is, countries of equal wealth, at least equal cultural and social development, and with a greater population will be subject to a global hegemon, just as the countries of Asia or the Middle East are, and as those of Africa would be if the United States could be bothered with them. NATO, despite the fine words, was never really a balanced partnership, but the present prospect would be much less balanced, and without the underlying necessity for the United States to manage the security of Europeans because of their weakness. Without countervailing balancers the United States will shape the international system in its own preferred form, which will reflect its own interests or perhaps the perceived interests of certain elements of the body politic. It goes without saying that that form would be greatly preferable to that which (say) the Soviet Union might have sought, or even that which (say) China might seek in the future. It does not follow by any means that it would be optimal, even for the United States in the long term. It is time for Europeans to act effectively in the international system, collectively and as individual national players, in a manner consistent with their wealth and level of development—in short, in accordance with their importance.

Thinking independently is not a hostile act. To engage and debate is not to be anti-American; indeed endeavoring to maintain a relationship that reflects the necessities and factors of half a century ago is far more likely to lead to tension in the longer term. As many American commentators have recognized, the only entity of any comparable weight to the United States in this century is likely to be the European Union. Since the United States, for understandable if not supportable reasons, will not take the lead in reforming the transatlantic relationships, the Europeans must.

CHAPTER FIVE

Whither Britain?

The question of transatlantic relations is more difficult for the United Kingdom than for any other European nation. History (often misunderstood), sentiment, and a false perspective and consciousness, not to mention strands of domestic politics and a strident press, make the calm identification and pursuit of national interests very difficult. So (paradoxically) does the relative improvement in the United Kingdom's economic and political stability since 1982. Successive governments have often been at pains to obscure the real issues and to proclaim, at best, the need to avoid choices. Unfortunately, the avoidance of choice, though sometimes a short-term necessity, is but seldom a basis for long-term strategy. It is now time for the United Kingdom to confront its actual position in the world, form a view about its long-term interests, and think about transatlantic relations in that context.

For fifty years from 1815 Britain was a highly successful state, economically, politically, militarily, and so diplomatically. That had indeed been true from some years before and continued to be so, to an extent (but a declining one), afterward. Despite the loss of the North American colonies, Britain was able to pursue a successful grand strategy. It had organized (and financed) coalitions to defeat the Napoleonic system, which had mobilized almost all Europe and its resources. It was able to order much of the world's commerce and trade, be the leading industrial country, be supreme in maritime matters, and acquire a second empire. At home, Britain undertook political reform that was felt at the time to have been successful (except in Ireland) and had a constitution that combined liberty with stability, despite the Chartist agitation, the Tolpuddle Martyrs, etc.[1] It was internationally in the top league, and in overall weight and influence it was second to none. British statesmen had for the most part a clear view of the national interest and how it should best be pursued.

The contrast with the situation at the beginning of the twenty-first century is acute. There has been a century of fumbling for a grand strategy; of losing economic momentum and then an empire; and of failure to effect necessary reforms, or at least of avoiding them for far too long. Most statesmen have scarcely been worthy of the name; those that were nevertheless contrived to make a series of mistakes the cumulative effect of which was devastating. They failed to define, much less pursue, rational national interests. Britain was less successful than France, or even Germany, in formulating and pursuing its ends in the twentieth century.[2] Indeed a major criticism is that it has not even tried; despite great potential advantages, it has since 1956—Suez—tended to cast its role and objective as that of the principal supporter of another power. Before Suez its twentieth-century grand strategy had sometimes been inept; afterward it became all but nonexistent, other than in nailing its colors to another country's mast.

From the early twentieth century onward Britain has suffered severe failures in defining desirable and attainable ends, and in using appropriate means to obtain them. The reasons for that are many and complex. Some have been unavoidable; others might have been circumvented by competent statecraft. Of course, all countries experienced difficulties with formulating appropriate strategies in the twentieth century. Part of the problem was the rise of democracy; diplomacy and, to a lesser extent, grand strategy in the ancien régime was almost entirely an aristocratic activity and skill. That is no longer acceptable—wider political awareness and engagement, a popular press, the rise of a superpower duopoly and then the collapse of one of its members, the phenomenon of globalization, and the increasing importance of nonstate actors have affected all players on the international stage and overtaken old-fashioned strategic thinking. The complexities of global trade, interwoven economies, and barely understood economic phenomena all make it difficult for any country to evolve a grand strategy, but stating the difficulties does not justify not attempting the task. Whether or not blame should attach to individuals or groups, the fact is that Britain for too long was on holiday from grand strategy. It is no longer able to indulge itself in that way. National and global interests alike demand a return to strategic thinking.

Grand strategy has itself undergone profound alteration. It is not, and never was, simply military; in the sixteenth century, fishing was promoted to provide England a source of hardy mariners; later the Navigation Acts were an intimate part of Britain's rise to commercial preeminence. By design or accident, the repeal of the Corn Laws not only enabled an industrial workforce to be fed cheaply but gave a major practical demonstration of the British economist David Ricardo's teachings on comparative advantage, encouraging Britain to concentrate on being the workshop of the world. Obviously, after the successes of the early industrial revolution, some falling back in Britain's relative position was inescapable as other countries developed. However, there were more profound problems than relative economic change. From the 1870s there was a clear failure to adapt the industries on which British prosperity had been built. Germany applied new technologies and indeed launched new industries, as did the United States.

By 1913 there was even a threat, in the event frustrated by revolution, from the seeming potential of Russian industry.

Fighting two debilitating world wars further undermined Britain's position. Whether or not either war could have been avoided, the fact was that by 1945 the British economy was in dire straits; politically the Empire had suffered major blows from enemies and allies, and the governing elite had lost faith in themselves and their mission. Statesmanship of the highest order would have been hard pressed to cope. Externally there were additional difficult changes in both Europe and Asia. However, no realistic reassessment of grand strategy took place. There was drift, and the best that can be said if it is that overall the military position in which Britain reached by 1957 was not inconsistent with the appropriate security posture for the Cold War. Politically and economically, the judgment would have to be far harsher. Repeated failure to address the world as it was and make necessary changes persisted in some spheres down to the 1980s, and in others until after 2000.

Whatever the pre-1945 failures, close alignment with the United States during the Cold War was understandable and to a large extent desirable. So long as that confrontation lasted, a reasonable judgment is that the United Kingdom's supreme interest was in retaining U.S. engagement in Europe and, within that, positions of British influence within NATO. With the end of the Cold War and the removal of the Soviet threat, different considerations apply. The costs of subordination became much more evident and the benefits far less. In any case, the desire to involve the United States focused upon the means rather than the end; now there is the need to consider both ends and means. It is time for Britain to set about rediscovering itself and once more identifying and pursuing its own interests.

That is not a plea for selfish unilateralism. A wide view of a nation's interests may well give great weight to the interests and concerns of others. There are good arguments for some merging of sovereignty, for putting significant resources at the disposal of others, and for accepting restrictions on what a nation does or can do. The point is that there should be the application of mind to facts to define objectives, analyze the consequences of particular policies and positions, and work out consequences—not simply unthinking followership.

Earlier chapters have outlined Churchill's hopes in 1945 for an enduring partnership with the United States. With the exception of Edward Heath, most of his successors followed a similar line (at any rate after 1956), however clear the gap in capabilities between Britain and the United States had become, and however clear therefrom that there could not be a partnership such as Churchill sought but a most unequal linkage. Politicians erected a new relationship, which they repeatedly referred to as a special relationship, even though the original of that had died at the end of the Second World War and though many influential players in Washington wished to disabuse the British.[3]

Margaret Thatcher in particular rejected, with visceral force, most things European and saw the world in terms of very close alignment with the United States. Her departure from the British political scene did not change things very much. Her successor, John Major, had a less wholehearted aversion to Europe, and his successor (Tony Blair) started with a strongly pro-European stance. However, that opening position was overtaken by events and by Tony Blair's close personal and political alignment with President Clinton and then by a different but in some ways even closer relationship with the second President Bush. The result was that the opening years of the twenty-first century saw the United Kingdom in very close support of the United States, politically and militarily.

In the period leading up to the 2003 Iraqi conflict the United Kingdom, as it had done for some years, continued to support the United States in air operations designed to protect the northern Kurds and the southern Shiite Arabs. On less dramatic matters it reportedly urged within the European Union (admittedly along with others, such as Greece) the U.S. line on the need for an early date for EU entry negotiations with Turkey. During 2002, despite the significant role the United Kingdom had played in the genesis of the ESDP, little British energy went into resuscitating that initiative as opposed to what was invested in rallying support for the United States over Iraq. As regards the Israel-Palestinian conflict, Britain, despite many reservations in official circles about the Israeli posture and actions, did not significantly distance itself from the American position and certainly did not seek to induce the EU to use its undoubted potential trade leverage over Israel.[4] When it came to fighting, Britain provided troops for combat roles in Afghanistan in 2001 and 2002, and it made a significant military contribution against Iraq in 2003.

Over that conflict, it gave strong and consistent political support to the United States, well ahead of any other major nation, markedly in front of almost all European states and far more than France and Germany, over the need to tackle Saddam Hussein. It was prepared to inflict grave damage on the EU (admittedly because, from a different perspective, France and Germany were also prepared to see damage inflicted) and to join with the United States in a war that met neither the classical criteria of a just war nor the requirements of the United Nations Charter as generally understood and that was not demanded as a matter of immediate prudence. From the U.S. initiatives, which the United Kingdom followed closely (although securing some important modifications in attempting to act through the UN), flowed damage to the United Nations and the international system, revelation of some grave fault lines in NATO, and loss of much British influence in the EU. The United Kingdom's positioning alongside the United

States probably undermined the British position in the Middle East for substantially more than a decade ahead.

At the beginning of 2003, despite some major reservations in the Labour Party over the specific question of military action against Iraq, there was little effective political challenge to the British government's general posture. The Conservative opposition appeared to support the government fully on the issue, as did most of the press. The government thus won divisions in the House of Commons despite significant Labour votes against.[5] Overall, there was little public opposition to the proposition that the United Kingdom should in almost all cases automatically support the United States and work closely with it. Nevertheless, there were and are real grounds for a reconsideration of that line.

In part the reasons why Britain needs at this stage to regain its ability to address strategic issues have to do with its role and position, or potential position, in the EU; at the same time, they arise from a strict examination of national interests. A balanced judgment requires an analysis of what the United Kingdom derives, directly and indirectly, and is likely to derive in future from such close, quasi-automatic, association. It also requires consideration of what price it is likely to have to pay for the benefits received, again directly and indirectly. In short, are the British people better or worse off for their very close following of the United States? All this, moreover, needs to be done for both the immediate and the longer-term future. The vital question is whether shaping a world beneficial for and to the United Kingdom is more likely to come about from automatic public locking-on to U.S. positions, or in some other way.

The Benefits

The potential direct benefits to the United Kingdom from continuing a very close association with the United States can be characterized as, on the one hand, helping to shape a world of the sort that would be beneficial to the United Kingdom—that is, acquiring and exercising influence with the United States so that the latter's great economic and political weight is, so far as possible, applied in ways that are helpful to the United Kingdom rather than otherwise. There is, on the other hand, the matter of strengthening the existing ties, which yield concrete benefits in the military and intelligence areas. The indirect benefits might include increasing the United Kingdom's general standing in the world, and hence its soft power.

Given that the United Kingdom, like other rich Western states, has many interests in common with the United States, there can be obvious advantages from pursuing those interests alongside it, since the latter has unmatched military power and preeminent political weight. That was, in a nutshell, the argument for U.S. leadership during the

Cold War—the British and other Europeans could secure their vital national interests only by the close and direct engagement of the United States in European security. What then benefited the United States usually benefited the Europeans too; the relatively few instances where that was not the case were outweighed by the essential general gains. However, with the subsequent shift in the nature of security and the development of differing national interests, perceived interests, and differing means of pursuing interests, that may no longer be the case.

Political Influence

The great difficulty is to know how much the United Kingdom benefits from a special, and in practice particularly subordinate, relationship with the United States.[6] That close involvement yields some influence is scarcely to be doubted. The issues to be addressed are how much of that intangible matter is gained at present from a close alignment; how much there may be in the future, and in what connections; and how important that which is gained actually is. In the other side of the scales must be placed the costs of gaining whatever benefit is to be had.

The buildup to the confrontation with Iraq saw a degree of multilateralism and UN involvement that was somewhat at odds with the picture of an administration determined on a unilateralist approach to the world. Some commentators ascribed the shift, or apparent shift, to the diplomacy and argumentation of the British prime minister. Unlike the French and German leaders, Mr. Blair gave public support to President Bush, but he is said to have argued the multilateral case in private. If changes could be put down to his intervention it would certainly add weight to the argument that the close relationship yielded influence. Whether, taking a long-term view, it yielded sufficient influence and more overall benefit to the United Kingdom than a different relationship would have done is, of course, a different matter. The instant assessment of the balance of close engagement shows that the United States was prepared when it could not get its way multilaterally to act as it thought fit, and it is difficult to see what immediate or longer-term benefits the United Kingdom derived by way of shaping the international system or resolving the Palestine/Israeli conflict.

It has been suggested that Tony Blair early on formed the judgment that it would be a severe setback if the United States were driven to act alone—the line, that is, that another voice at the table, even in an unequal partnership, would be preferable to pure American unilateralism. Just why that should be so is not clear; if the result is an action that would have been taken unilaterally in any case, there seems no advantage in masking, to a small extent, its unilateral nature. Support of the United States won some favorable regard for Blair and the United Kingdom in that country, but the tangible advantages of that regard remain to be demonstrated. Meanwhile, the political costs elsewhere have been very real.

It is possible, of course, that speaking out could have led to a loss of influence in Washington, in which case the United States would have pursued a purely unilateral course, with even greater damage to the international system and British (and other) interests within that. That is, the best attainable outcome may have been that, by compromising its own immediate interests, Britain influenced the United States to a greater extent than would otherwise have been the case. It is difficult to ascertain whether that has been the case in particular instances, not only because it is difficult to gauge what effect British intervention had in Washington but because a clear definition of British interests has been lacking.

Whatever the precise balance of advantage and cost of the support for the Iraq war may be, what is necessary in ascertaining the appropriateness of this aspect of U.S.-British relations is judgment as to whether the giving and accepting of counsel necessarily involves the subordination of the pursuit of British interests to public acquiescence in American views. Clearly the Bush administration has been most unwilling to accept public criticism, as shown in its reactions to the French and German positions on the Iraq conflict. The question is, however, whether it would have moved, to a greater or lesser extent than it did, in the direction desired by Tony Blair if he had made it clear that unless there was substantial movement he would not support the president and his war. Since as it was the administration could take his public support for granted, it is not clear what negotiating leverage the United Kingdom had in this particular instance.[7]

More generally, as chapters 3 and 4 above indicate, significant British influence over U.S. actions or policies is not unknown but has been rare and may be becoming rarer. All indications are that in the future it will become rarer yet. If that is so, privy counsel may produce little benefit for the United Kingdom and so justify little subordination of interests. It is, for example, possible that Britain has weakened its standing in Europe or in the Middle East by acquiescing to Washington on issues where speaking out would have yielded greater soft power in the long term, and where, in any case, at the end of the day, it has had no perceptible influence on the actual U.S. policy outcomes.

Military Cooperation

The benefits to the United Kingdom from its close association with the United States are easiest to ascertain in the military area. The Ministry of Defence has studied the matter and quantified the benefits. They are most obvious in respect of major weapons systems. For example, producing itself a missile system with the capabilities of Trident would have been well beyond the United Kingdom's economic strength. Submarine-launched cruise missiles can be purchased from the United States for a fraction of the sum that would have been required for their domestic development. At a lower level, the common servicing of Trident missiles at a U.S. facility saves the United Kingdom very substantial sums. (If nuclear testing were ever resumed, the United Kingdom would have no site of its own at which to do it.) In other words, the United Kingdom has had very large tangible benefits from its military association with the United States, and without them it would have less effective systems or fewer capabilities, or a much higher defense budget.

There are also other significant operational benefits from the two countries' armed forces acting together. The Royal Air Force is well ahead of other European air forces in what it can do and how it does it. The benefits for the Royal Navy's working abilities have been even greater; during the Cold War it operated at a technical and professional level surpassed, and that only in parts, by the U.S. Navy. The issues for the future are whether such benefits will be needed and available, and if so whether they will be dependent upon something like the earlier intimate and "special" relationship, and at what price in political autonomy. Such questions go to the heart of what the United Kingdom will wish to do militarily and how that will compare with the concerns of the United States; they also raise major issues of defense industrial policy on both sides of the Atlantic.

On that latter, the close relationship with the United States yields considerable benefit to British defense industries. U.S. policy is notoriously obstructive and protectionist in this area, but the limited attempts to free it up have benefited British companies, with which American collaboration is closer than with most others. BAE, for example, had U.S. sales of $4,000 million in 2001. Some of this sort of relationship would continue without the close political relations between governments, but the possibility of moving or diminishing the formidable barriers would be less without the political collaboration. At the same time, it must be admitted that all the closeness has not moved the American position very far; transatlantic military trade is still very much a one-way street; all European companies together account for only 3 percent of the U.S. defense market.[8]

Intelligence Cooperation

British-U.S. cooperation in the intelligence field has been important since the Second World War; both sides have benefited greatly, though it is not easy to quantify the benefits in financial terms. A degree of quantification was, in principle, easier when security depended, for example, very heavily on satellites and the United Kingdom benefited from "overhead" collection on a scale that it could not have afforded itself. Today the relationship also involves intimate working relationships and exchanges of analysis and interpretation on a privileged basis. The benefits with respect to how the United

Kingdom's armed forces are able to operate were extraordinarily great during the Cold War and remain very valuable.

The relationship still gives access to data that the United Kingdom could not have collected without expenditure on an inconceivable scale; what may have changed is the relevance of some of that intelligence. Before September 2001 the United States was not preeminently well geared to the forms of collection best calculated to help in countering terrorism or other items on the new security agenda. Indeed, because the contributions of U.S. intelligence to the problems of the new security agenda are less preeminent, it now has much more to gain from collaboration with others. The habits of working together, both on collection and interpretation, fostered over the years can still be of particular benefit to the United Kingdom, which would be most unlikely to consider foregoing the benefits so long as they were on offer.

The Costs of Collaboration

The obvious costs of particularly close collaboration with the United States are of two main sorts: firstly, dependence on the United States and the consequent need to conform to its policies, doctrines, and ways of doing things, which may not be the most appropriate for meeting the United Kingdom's needs; and secondly, loss or impairment of influence in Europe and more widely. The second sort was demonstrated by the results of the close association in early 2003 with the United States over the lead-up to and consequences of war with Iraq. The divisions between the United Kingdom on the one side, and France and Germany on the other, may well have put back the possibility of an effective CFSP for many years. Certainly they undermined in the short term any claim by Britain to a leading role in determining EU foreign policy and gravely damaged attempts by the Union to forge more coherent and effective policies.[9]

The first sort of cost includes the fact that often in the British policy-making process there is the explicit desire to avoid crossing the U.S. line; particular groups may press for a course not on the basis of British interests but because it commends itself to the United States. Thus senior naval officers may wish the United Kingdom to avoid policies that would be at variance with those favored by the U.S. Navy, because of the close working relationship with the latter. For example, even modest post–Cold War proposals from a dependable ally for collaboration on submarines were difficult for the United Kingdom because of U.S. classification sensitivities. Again, at a time when the Conventional Forces in Europe arms control negotiations were proceeding apace but American naval officers were very resistant to applying any such measures to their own assets, senior British officers felt an acute need not to differ. Correcting that sort of tendency requires political and official effort and, even more crucially, awareness of when such a distorting factor arises.

Another aspect of this group of costs is the framing of procurement and doctrinal decisions along lines that are designed to fit in with the United States and its interests rather than the United Kingdom's own needs. If a country wishes to influence the United States in military decisions, it has to be able to fight alongside American forces. Since the end of the Vietnam War, the United Kingdom has shown a desire to collaborate with the United States in almost all of its major military activities outside Southeast Asia, although not to participate in its minor interventions in the Western Hemisphere (e.g., Grenada, Panama, or Haiti). It has been a most steadfast proponent of "NATO First" and of the need for U.S. engagement in European security. It has seen its likely major military deployments as coalition operations with U.S. leadership.

European nations need to deliberate very carefully on what military tasks they are likely to need to undertake and how they will undertake them. This applies with particular force to the United Kingdom, because of its close military involvement with the United States and its clearly expressed desire to maintain a large degree of interoperability with it. Even in the cases when the Americans' policy is wise, the means they favor for implementing it may well not be suited to the capabilities and preferences of junior partners. Engagement with the United States may therefore cause problems, not least in terms of the levels and especially the nature of defense expenditure, if a partner wishes to be interoperable. This may not have been a significant problem for the United Kingdom so far, but it will very probably become so in the near future. There seems no likelihood that the United States will turn away from seeking high-technology solutions to military problems or from spending on a scale that no other society will match.

More generally, the costs of dependence involve the risk of the Americans' turning off a supply of materiel or intelligence. A suggestion of the difficulties that would be likely to arise could be seen when, during the post-Yugoslavian tensions in the Balkans, U.S. intelligence was withdrawn from coalition operations, not because of policy differences with the United Kingdom but because of congressional unwillingness to see an arms embargo enforced. A more significant lesson could be drawn from the 1956 Suez imbroglio, where the vital resource withheld to frustrate independent British policies was support for the pound sterling. France drew from that episode the lesson that it should never be dependent on the United States; the United Kingdom drew the very different conclusion that it must never act without American support. The former may not have been correct in the context of the Cold War; the latter may not be appropriate in the very different post–Cold War era. There seems to be no evidence that cutoffs of materiel or intelligence have been threatened to gain British acquiescence in U.S. policies in recent years, but perhaps there has been no need even to threaten that, since British acquiescence for most U.S. policies has been so readily forthcoming. If the United Kingdom joined more closely with a Europe that resisted American policies more often, perhaps matters would change; there could be an opportunity cost for the United Kingdom in being seen as more or less automatically following Europe rather than America. All of that demonstrates that receiving substantial U.S. military and intelligence benefits is not cost free.

All states err from time to time, and the repercussions of American errors are by virtue of the nation's size likely to be great, particularly on smaller and weaker players. The United States may pursue courses that are not in its own best interests, let alone those of other nations. Some countries may have no alternative but to follow larger ones; for those who have an option, the risk of entanglement in mistaken policies needs to be weighed with care. In any case, those that could enjoy wider options must think of providing themselves the wherewithal to act when the United States does not wish to do so, whether for good or bad reasons. Much of that applies to larger European countries generally; some applies with particular force to the United Kingdom, because its political and military structures and habits give it wider options than, say, Germany enjoys. Such thinking underlay the St. Malo initiative, where the British prime minister was apparently concerned that as regards Kosovo the United States would not act and the Europeans at that stage could not. He correctly saw the need for the Europeans, who had the economic resources, to fit themselves for at least a degree of independent military action.

Britain in Europe

Despite having missed and made a mess of many opportunities for assuming a leading role in Europe, and despite continuing Euro-skepticism, the United Kingdom is likely to remain a member of the EU and to strive to increase its influence there. Britain's ability to secure what it wants within what is undoubtedly the most important international forum for its general well-being is and will be influenced by the perceptions of other European governments (and peoples) of its activities and commitments. Standing aside from the generality of European opinion will therefore in itself bring a price. That price may be the impairment of the EU's development or of the United Kingdom's role in Europe, or both. Such a price may be tolerable, even necessary, but it will be real. It must be offset against the benefits that close shadowing of U.S. policies may bring.

Notwithstanding enlargement, the predominant political and much of the economic weight within the European Union remains in the original founder members, especially France and Germany, who opposed in common the U.S. line on Iraq in 2003. Each has significant domestic political and economic problems, and in different ways each has failed to implement reform in the economic sphere. There is no ready way in which the United Kingdom can find extensive early common ground with them to reform the EU's internal business or to move it forward as an international actor. France is keen for there to be a major European voice in the world but wishes it to have a French accent. Despite great willingness to collaborate with the United Kingdom on military matters, it has in recent years sought to reinvigorate a Franco-German axis in which it has the preponderant voice and to diminish opportunities for British influence, seemingly concerned not only about British links with the United States but also that an increase in British influence in the EU would limit its own. Germany is still unsure of itself as a major diplomatic or military actor outside Europe.

Whatever the strength of the arguments that the United Kingdom should seek to reinforce European capabilities, and they are considerable, London does not have a simple option of turning from an American engagement to a European one, where it would be welcomed with open arms. In any case, whatever the opportunities for Britain to have made a role for itself in Europe half a century ago, the effluxion of time has closed off many options. Nevertheless, the arguments for Britain's focusing on its own influence within the EU are very strong. There is a commonality of interests and approaches, as well as economic benefits, all pointing to the need to maximize rather than diminish British influence there.

Closeness to the United States may, of course, affect Britain's role in Europe in a positive sense, even if it weakens the country's ability to influence some fellow members of the EU on foreign policy issues. In military matters it undoubtedly gives an edge to Britain's ability to play a leading role in European defense; it may help with influence with some newer members, though to the extent that they incline toward a U.S. line that is likely to be a result of their direct contact with the United States, not their approval of a British stance. However, more generally, there is evidence that such closeness has hampered Britain's ability to play a role in Europe. That has operated both on outside actors, as in Charles de Gaulle's rejection of the United Kingdom because of its American links and in the inhibition of British officials and ministers in looking to Europe as they seek to maintain and reinforce transatlantic ties. Nevertheless, nothing suggests that the United Kingdom's core interests differ significantly from those of other major European states. If there are constant divergences of Britain's policies from those of, say, France or Germany, the question of why that is so must surely arise. The causes and justification for the differences must be looked into; even if there are good objective grounds for them, the penalty that they bring in terms of diminution of British influence in the European Union and of EU influence in the world must be weighed against the direct gains from the pursuit of an American orientation.

What such an orientation requires can, of course, be subject to change. There have over the years been shifts in the U.S. attitude toward European integration and Britain's place in that. In the 1940s and for long after, the pressure from Washington was toward deeper European integration, including that of Britain. At present the prevailing view in Washington seems against integration and toward picking partners for coalitions of the willing. Certainly there is now no suggestion from that quarter that the United Kingdom should pursue deeper European engagement. Washington appears to have taken the view that its interests will be served by preventing not only the emergence of any hostile power that could oppose it but even a Europe coherent and unified in diplomatic and security issues. Having long opposed separate European security structures, it now apparently seeks in addition to divide Europeans, that it may more easily assert its way generally. For Britain as an EU member, the working out of such policies can only pose continual embarrassment, aside from impediments to its own interests (unless those are defined as always following the U.S. lead).

To Choose or Not to Choose

It has been a long-standing maxim of British policy that the country must avoid a fundamental choice between Europe and America. Mrs. Thatcher implicitly, and to an extent explicitly, rejected that while in office; she was more forthright after her fall from power, when she became very clear about the choice that should be made—that is, in favor of the United States. It must be considered whether the maxim is any longer a useful or even a safe guide to policy. A choice should not be lightly made, and there should be no rejection of the American pole purely for reasons of national assertion, along the lines of Gaullist policy in France. Nevertheless, it is time to address two questions openly and honestly. Firstly, is the current prime minister's assumption that Britain must automatically position itself with the United States and seek to be closer to it than any other country reasonable, feasible, or desirable? Secondly, should and does Britain's future lie in Europe, and if so, does that mean that avoiding a fundamental choice is an outmoded rule? Is avoiding choice a tenable position?

In his address to British ambassadors in January 2003, the prime minister argued that Britain must be at the center of Europe and that to separate itself from Europe would be madness. However, he also argued that the first principle of foreign policy is that Britain should remain the closest ally of the United States. It is not easy to see how his desire that Britain should be at the heart of Europe can be accomplished if London's first foreign policy aim is to be the closest ally of the United States. His argument does not make clear why the latter must be an absolute, what the benefits are, or why they will always outweigh the costs, no matter what price the United States asks.

The prime minister indeed asserted that Britain's European and American roles reinforce each other—that Britain could be a transatlantic bridge. There are severe limits to such a metaphor, however, not least that a bridge generally links two fixed points, not moving, developing, and interacting entities. More importantly, it is not clear how the prime minister can assert that Britain has one enduring interest—being the closest ally of the United States—and that (by strong implication) that interest is entirely in the United Kingdom's hands and should be pursued whatever the cost. The correct answer to the first question must surely be, as Lord Palmerston pointed out a century and a half ago, that Britain has enduring interests rather than enduring friends. There are great advantages to be had from a close relationship with the United States, but that should never be an absolute; the national interest must be weighed occasion by occasion, or at least from time to time.

As regards the second question, the European Union has many weaknesses and many failings. However, geography, history, and the working of the international system indicate that Britain's long-term interests are likely to be better served as an influential part of an effective EU than in pursuing them alone. Most objective observers would agree on that, however much they might differ on the details and eventual extent of EU integration. Here the choice is not between joining Europe and becoming effectively the fifty-first of the United States; it is between joining Europe and being an outside petitioner of the United States, receiving some benefits, at some cost and without a major voice in the determination of U.S. policy.

Striking the Balance

Time and again, it has been possible to see the United Kingdom following a U.S. line where there was no direct benefit to the United Kingdom and where the indirect benefits are so indirect as to be invisible. The Middle East is perhaps the clearest example of that, whether over Israel/Palestine or Iraq.[10] Whether considered on objective grounds of what is likely to secure a just and lasting peace or on grounds of national self-interest, there is nothing to be said for the United Kingdom's hesitation to condemn and take appropriate action against the illegal activities of Israel. Nevertheless, the United Kingdom has blocked even mild European action on that and, despite pressing the U.S. president to agree to the publication of the quadripartite "road map," has not spoken out clearly against the long-running and consistent American bias on the matter.[11]

As regards Iraq, the United Kingdom undoubtedly shared with the United States a common (if mistaken) view, based on intelligence reporting, of Saddam Hussein's doings and misdoings over a long period. He headed an evil regime that had sought and continued to seek weapons of mass destruction. He had also used such weapons, though not against any well-armed Western power from which retaliation might have been expected. Early statements from the Bush administration in 2002 ignored the most obvious questions that would arise from an attempt to change the regime.[12] It is possible, though far from certain, that Mr. Blair's diplomacy was a factor in the administration's later more sensible and fleshed-out approach. It did not, however, stop a move to war with a now-notorious absence of preparations to secure the peace. It is, moreover, a question whether the United Kingdom's standing in the world at large and in Europe was enhanced by such strong expressions of solidarity, and in due course demonstrations of it by joining in the war, when others were much more reluctant and there was a pressing need to build up the role and relevance of the United Nations and of a rule-based international system. The current system is not an unchanging given; a major aspect of any choice is its making or remaking. At present, the unilateral American attitudes, military power, and political influence mean that in many ways the United States *is* the system. However, a unipolar system cannot be counted upon to remain either stable or benign over time.

Even if the prime minister's private interventions with the president can be credited with helping guide the latter to the UN route in late 2002, there is a strong case that given the earlier incoherent thinking on Iraq in the United States and the lack of any likely immediate threat to any Western country, and notwithstanding the short, militarily successful, and not too destructive initial intervention, Britain's actions and words damaged rather than enhanced its general position. Also, it is not clear what benefits they brought and bought with respect to the United States that would not have been available to a somewhat more distant interlocutor.

Even if it be admitted that the United Kingdom has from time to time a significant impact on American policy, that impact is likely, even with administrations less unilateralist in outlook than the second Bush one, to be less decisive than the effect that the United Kingdom could have upon policy formation in Europe, where it is dealing with states of broadly its own size and weight. It may be objected that Britain could never equal either France or Germany in political impact in Europe. That may be true in the short term, given the United Kingdom's long history of standing aside (not to say obstruction), its manifestly close association with the policies of a non-European power, and the special factors affecting the Franco-German couple. However, globally, the United Kingdom has more weight than either France or Germany alone over a range of issues, and there it can have a major impact, as the St. Malo initiative showed. Clear commitment to Europe and the addition of Britain's weight to carrying forward the EU's development, would increase the British role and the country's ability to affect the formulation of European policy.

It may be objected that the EU is a political and military lightweight, that major impact on its policy formation is of less effect than a small impact on U.S. policy making. That is true, but it is not the whole truth. There are several important glosses to be made. Firstly, the EU is an *economic* heavyweight, and influencing the development of its economic policies is of real national interest to the United Kingdom and can serve its interests in the wider world. While the United States in principle believes in open markets and free trade, its particular economic policies in practice very much (understandably) serve its own interests; there is a long history of damage to British interests from those policies. Secondly, while the EU does indeed have far to go in developing coherent and effective foreign policy, there is every indication that the world needs alternatives to a unilateralist U.S. hegemonic approach. British and wider interests would therefore be better served were the United Kingdom to put its weight and influence into making the European Union a proper strategic and diplomatic actor rather than simply reinforcing, almost automatically, American policies. Even if Britain's every immediate economic and military want could be met by adhering to the United States it would be wrong to do that, neglecting the development of Europe, because in time the United Kingdom would end up taking whatever policies the United States handed out, and in due course it would find an international system forged by U.S. policies and by the reactions of China, India, or the Muslim world against them. Only by the wildest chance could that system meet Britain's long-term requirements.

In short, effort put into strengthening the weaker foreign policy entity, where British input might on occasion be decisive or at least very influential, would in the present state of the world be a better investment than attempting to temper or steer the doings of an actor who feels itself so strong that it will ultimately seek its own ends almost irrespective of the needs or arguments of others.

There is another aspect to all this, much less easily voiced in the United Kingdom (and with even greater difficulty in England) than in France or even Italy or Spain—national pride or feelings of worth. Britain is chauvinistic and has a chauvinistic press. However, that chauvinism is very rarely, if ever, displayed toward one power, to which British policies are regularly subordinated and the policies of which are so strongly maintained that the United Kingdom can have little impact upon them. It is highly undesirable to encourage chauvinism or anti-Americanism. However, a reasonable pride in England, Britain, and Europe, their political and cultural achievements, and a sense of the great many good things that have come thence (as well as some bad ones) might reasonably lead to a feeling that a position of perpetual subordination to American whims and prejudices is no good thing, any more than subordination to French or German ones would be. In urging that, one does not need to uphold uncritically some unhistorical view of the state or the nation-state in all its alleged post-Westphalian or nineteenth-century sovereignty. One need do no more than suggest that a reasonable feeling of sympathy with one's own group and its values has a role to play. Groups or entities called England, Britain, and the United Kingdom exist. They form parts of larger wholes, in which they should have appropriate voices. Sometimes they represent a collection of views or aspirations that can best be considered on their own merits. Often they function most effectively with partners. At the very least, partnerships should be freely chosen on their merits, partnerships that will usually involve a true community of interests and a sharing of authority.

The French, perhaps for the wrong reasons—after all *le soldat* Chauvin was a (mythical) Frenchman—recognized that at an early stage. For reasons connected with their different fates and roles in the Second World War, and with Churchill's part in that conflict and his relationship with Roosevelt, the British did not do so and have not done so yet. Sixty-five years after a war in which Britain's only hope of avoiding defeat was linkage with the United States, the time has surely come to consider again whether the maxims of almost all earlier statesmen, and indeed of Churchill himself before 1939, may not provide useful alternative guidance for the coming century. Obviously, the past cannot be a complete guide to the future; certain things have changed for ever. The world of the twenty-first century is not that of William Pitt (Elder or Younger), Lord Castlereagh, Palmerston, or the Marquis of Salisbury. Equally, it is not that of Churchill, Bevin, or Thatcher. Britain has to address the world as it is, to consider how it might better shape that world to its tastes and interests. In a world that has changed very greatly in less than two decades, maxims forged in the last sixty years of the twentieth century should be regarded as no more persuasive than those applied from 1700 to 1914. All may have something to teach; none is likely to provide a golden key to every question.

The United States has indeed done much good; it has also done considerable harm, and the views of many leading Americans as to the universality of its way of doing and understanding things are unhistorical and need to be seen as the creatures of a particular time and place. Great as is the weight of the United States, it has not found unique truth or virtue. It should be a valued partner, not an automatic choice for Britain, irrespective of other claims. With little objective justification, 1776 saw the rupturing of one set of ties between Britain and what became the United States. It is now time, with much more justification, to end the present links and forge new and more wholesome ones based on a true view of interests and a desire for cordial cooperation rather than control and direction.

On any view, in economic, military, political, and cultural matters, the United States will be a major part of the world that Britain faces. Cooperation with it will often be beneficial. Nevertheless, demographically and increasingly economically, the United States will, as the twenty-first century progresses, be a smaller part of the whole. Politically, the effect of a single overwhelming, unipolar, conventional military capability will diminish as new, "asymmetric" threats arise in response or reaction to it and as new security challenges to which it provides no answers become ever more apparent.

Britain has and will have interests that are distinct from those of the United States, and it will need to find partners appropriate to the pursuit of those interests. Sometimes the right partner, alone or with others, will be the United States; often the appropriate partners will be other Europeans; sometimes extra-European links will be important (and sometimes extra-European players will seek partners who are not the United States simply to avoid its overweening influence).

All this is no more than a call for the United Kingdom to apply (mutatis mutandis) to itself the approaches that the United States unhesitatingly applies to its own national interest. It does not imply a rejection of the United States, much less of the important values enshrined in some of the latter's founding documents. It does imply independent thought about the interests of those who live within the United Kingdom and of those in the wider world. It must involve consideration of the wider entities of which, by reason of history and geography and political decisions, the United Kingdom forms a part.

CHAPTER SIX

New Relationships for Old

No nation is to be trusted farther than it is bound by its interest; and no prudent statesman or politician will venture to depart from [this maxim].

'Tis folly for one Nation to look for disinterested favors from another. . . . There can be no greater error than to expect, or calculate upon real favours from Nation to Nation.

The course of this nation does not depend on the decisions of others.

Without U.S. military and economic involvement, Britain and Western Europe would not have survived the Second World War in recognizable form; without such involvement during the Cold War they might well not have survived the challenge of Soviet oppression and dictatorship.

The Past

When it finally entered the Second World War, the United States provided not only the arsenal of democracy but also many fighting men in the European theater, and a great preponderance of them in the Pacific. It provided both credit and munitions to a Britain that neither had the one nor could produce the other in sufficient quantity, and it helped keep supplies going to the Soviet Union. After the war, despite history and its internal pressures toward isolationism and unilateralism, the United States played a major role in making the world system. It was, with some limitations, a multilateral actor, joining in a profoundly important transatlantic partnership. U.S. financial power relaunched Western Europe and then its engagement throughout the Cold War; the Americans protected that area and also ensured the eventual freedom of Central and Eastern Europe, and indeed ultimately made possible that of Russia itself. All Europeans, therefore, have much for which to thank America.

In doing all that the United States, of course, also served its own vital interests. Roosevelt recognized the challenge from Nazi Germany, and he was greatly concerned lest the British fleet fall into German hands. At first he hoped to hold off the threat by supporting France and Britain. Even when it became clear that the defeat of the Third Reich by Britain alone was most unlikely, the United States was not moved to enter the war directly and fully; Japan's attack and Hitler's declaration of war were required for that. During the Cold War, facing what was seen as a worldwide challenge from a potentially global actor, Washington saw that its vital interests would have been seriously undermined if the relatively rich and developed states of Western Europe were to fall to the Soviet empire. Hence there was a shared vital interest in direct American involvement in European security.

The resulting transatlantic regime was thus based on American support for Europe against a Soviet threat and was, for a large part of the postwar period, manifested by a large U.S. military presence in Europe. The link, embodied in and demonstrated by the North Atlantic Alliance, gave rise to the sense that the relationship of the United States with Europe was different from relations with other parts of the world. Over time there came to be emphasis on a community of values, liberal or democratic, as well as shared security interests. The rhetoric on shared values was sometimes more evident than the substance. At times of considerable domestic repression both Portugal and Turkey were able to be members of NATO (though Spain was not admitted during the Franco era—which did not prevent bilateral U.S. defense arrangements with that country). Nevertheless, the polarization with the Soviet Union did give reality to talk of democracy, freedom, and a genuine shared security, involving values as well as territory. When that threat dissipated it was not clear why Europe should still want U.S. engagement in its security, either physically or by way of guarantee. Attempts to spell out the need, such as NATO's "Strategic Concepts" of 1991 and 1999, were not convincing; they were rhetoric rather than demonstration. The truth perhaps lay in a word heard more often in academic than in diplomatic circles—unipolarity. Since there was one and only one all-powerful actor, the United States, there was at least a supposition that it would need to cope with almost all significant security threats; expressed somewhat differently, if the United States was the indispensable power, it should clearly continue to be the key in European security.

The actual and substantive change in transatlantic relations brought about by the collapse of the Soviet Union was obscured for a while by a number of factors. Firstly, almost all parties continued to say (for whatever reason) how necessary U.S. involvement was. Secondly, the Europeans showed themselves incapable, despite their wealth, of dealing with the military and political issues that arose in the former Yugoslavia. (In part, they were self-deterred—they lacked the confidence that they could manage the situation as it turned difficult. In part, however, they simply lacked sufficient capacity in the necessary military capabilities.) However, by the beginning of the twenty-first century, particularly in the light of the Kosovo war (1999) and of the preparations for a second conflict with Iraq, the differences were manifest between what the United States could and would do and what most of the Europeans believed the appropriate ways of tackling problems. The Kosovo operation was declared a success, and in a technical sense it was, but the mutual loss of confidence across the Atlantic, as well as the demonstration of weaknesses in NATO's means of doing things, probably made it the first and last war of the Alliance as such.

Arrangements that gave a necessary primacy to the United States were understandable in the period immediately after the Second World War. Only that country had the economic and military strength to start renewal and safeguard security in Europe. Moreover, so long as the Soviet Union existed, with its vast armed forces and great arsenal of nuclear weapons, the need for deep U.S. engagement in European security was palpable. However, with the collapse of the Soviet Union, growth in the economic strength of Western European states, and an increase in the impact of the European Union, the case for that engagement was much diminished and the role of the transatlantic link much less clear. Nevertheless, because of its military and economic (and so political) strength, the United States must figure very largely in the operation of the international system, or rather systems, and so also in the foreign relations of European states. The question is *how* should it figure.

The Present

U.S. engagement in Europe and elsewhere must be seen in the perspective of earlier history, going back to the American Revolution. More than in any European country, the political legacy of two hundred years ago is alive and flourishing in the United States. American unwillingness to be subordinated to any outside power or influence marks a real divide across the Atlantic. The feeling of exceptionalism, drawn originally from Protestant rhetoric, is a factor not found in even the most Protestant of European countries. Moreover, while the strong private charitable currents within the United States impart to the nation a desire to do good, to help the poor and afflicted, outside its boundaries, they tend to define the good that it wishes to do very narrowly; there is a general American tendency to identify worthy and unworthy actors and recipients. Shades of gray are not usually part of the analysis.

Much the same is true of the U.S. government as an actor, and its policies are subject to a degree of influence by internal pressure groups not frequently found elsewhere. All governments understandably place their own national interests first, but in Europe at any rate there is a marked and growing tendency to subordinate the national to supranational or international requirements. There is little observable inclination to do that in the United States; indeed, there has been a recent tendency to back away from even self-imposed or negotiated restraints of international law. Moreover, the feeling of exceptionalism leads frequently to a desire to export what are seen as the American virtues and values; a strong school of so-called neoconservatives seeks to remold the world in what it perceives as the American image, spreading political democracy and economic liberalism. It does not hesitate to advocate the use of armed force to that end in certain cases.

Since the end of the Cold War there have been, and with the second Bush administration there now are, real questions as to what sort of actor the United States will be. The instincts of the principal makers of policy lean toward unfettered primacy and rejection of even the lightest of outside constraints. U.S. political weight can indeed ensure that many desirable things happen. Equally, it can prevent the coming about of many things, for good or ill, possibly frustrating others' security or economic objectives. Nevertheless, it seems clear to almost all outsiders that neither in international economics nor in current security needs is the United States likely to achieve its ends if it acts alone.

In establishing global order, neither Asia, with the exception of Australasia (and, in a limited sphere, Japan) nor Africa will yield much help to the United States in either the security or the economic spheres. Europe and the United States have much more in common. There is almost bound to remain a different relationship with Europeans than with other parts of the world in tackling global issues, even if the tasks are to be tackled in an essentially unilateral way.

Europe needs the United States for the same essential reasons as the United States needs Europe—to help consolidate and safeguard a liberal world order. At present, and above all, to the extent that the application of military force is a necessary part of that safeguarding, Europe needs the United States because the former is not, and its component states are not, capable of fighting a serious military campaign beyond the borders.

A further current reason for U.S. engagement in European security structures is to act as a check and lever. That, of course, runs both ways: engaged, the United States may check and influence European policies; however, a United States directly involved in a multilateral framework may be less likely to be able to pursue its own policies without regard to the needs and interests of others. However, such leverage will be more and more difficult to achieve in practice, since the United States shows so little willingness to subordinate itself to allies in the interests of alliance solidarity.

While all countries have a general interest in peace and economic development, there will be in a complex world differences of interests and, even more, of perceived interests. Peace at what price, and with what risks? Whose economic development, and on what terms? These are questions that constantly arise. American governments will seek to pursue their own interests, which may or may not be coincident with those of other countries. An objective view does not suggest that the United States is either always on the wrong side or always on the right; its governments are both as fallible and as likely to be right as any others. However, since Washington needs, in many areas, to take so little notice of the requirements of others, it may pursue policies that have an adverse effect elsewhere in a way that states that have to be more responsive to international opinion cannot. Despite assertions of American primacy and the need to maintain it, perpetual subordination of the judgments or interests of others to those of the United States can be justified on the basis of neither history nor principle. Some subordination may indeed be necessary and so appropriate in particular cases, but the need has to be judged in the light of all the circumstances.

There are a range of problems in the face of which Europe as a whole cannot yet stand on its own feet, much less be an effective leader for others. The underlying lack is of political weight and military capability. Similar problems affect the individual European states too.

First of all, the EU is not a nation-state; it does not have one foreign policy. It has some common policies but no comprehensive ones; meanwhile, its constituent members, retaining and guarding jealously their power and individual authority in many areas of foreign affairs, also have their own. Even worse, the EU lacks coherence in policy formation; its machinery is not effective in its parts, and there is a lack of coordination between the different organs. Responsibilities are divided between the Council and the Commission, and there is no satisfactory mechanism for articulation between them. All this will be made worse by enlargement, despite the efforts to produce and adopt a constitutional treaty.

Even if the EU could somehow formulate effective foreign policies, it would do so in vain in many areas, because it lacks capabilities, especially but not only military ones, to give effect to them. The Union has advanced to expressing the desire for a modest level of military capabilities but not to providing the necessary resources. Even if those were forthcoming, there would still be a lack of policy for their use. Above all, linked with the incoherence of policy formation but not identical with it, there is a lack of will to do what is necessary as a major political actor on the world stage—in particular, to use force.

Europe collectively has become inward looking, and some European states have become isolationist, in the sense of bounding their horizons by the immediate geographical area. Europe is unable to protect its interests in the world or to make the impact that it should, considering its wealth, culture, geography, and history. There is a need (and, despite the many problems, some opportunity) to rectify that and for Europe to grow up. That would be healthy for Europe itself, for the international system, and so for the world in general. In the medium and longer terms, it would even be good for America.

The opportunity lies in the absence of overwhelming, or indeed almost any, threat of conventional war to Europe. During the Cold War, the imperative was to face the Soviet Union; that required territorial defense, heavy U.S. engagement, and subordination of many local policies to keeping the United States engaged and providing a credible defense. Europe still needs friends and collaborators to deal with the new security agenda and, more generally, to promote its interests, but others need Europe as much. Even the United States needs Europe, if it is to promote a liberal economic agenda, pursue terrorists, promote Western values, and undertake political and economic development in backward areas.

On the other hand, that opportunity is limited by the post–11 September American obsession with doing what it wants in its own way—not least in waging the "war on terror." Until the 2000 Bush administration, the United States was reasonably supportive of developments in EU foreign and security policies, though there had long been major hesitation about any degree of European autonomy in military matters. Of Europe's heavyweights, the United Kingdom, its leading military power, had changed tack and was supportive of the development of an ESDP, which indeed had sprung from an Anglo-French initiative in 1998. France was pulling in the right direction. Only Germany was lagging. That state of affairs was deteriorating markedly by the start of 2003, largely over the U.S. initiatives on Iraq; the actual outbreak of war resulted in a major setback for the development of European policies. The emphasis on military solutions relying on strengths that are peculiarly America's own and the rejection of other opinions and approaches make it difficult for European or any other actors to pursue different strategies, even though the same factors point to the need to hear other voices and to the necessity for Europeans to get their act together.

The United Kingdom continued to align itself very closely with the United States over Iraq—indeed, the prime minister made general close alignment a rule of policy, not simply a pragmatic matter flowing from the facts of particular cases. Public opinion in Europe was much more reserved. France and Germany celebrated the fortieth anniversary of the Elysée Treaty (the Franco-German Friendship Treaty of 22 January 1963) by an attempted relaunch of their axis within the EU—an undertaking largely directed, it appeared, against U.S. policies and probably British influence in Europe. Germany asserted that it would not take part in any war and, with France and Belgium, refused to agree to NATO planning for sending military aid to Turkey to help repel any attack on it following a U.S. strike on Iraq. In riposte, eight EU countries (including the United Kingdom) came out in support of the United States. In short, there was no common

EU position on the major crisis of the time, no prospect of any, and little effort to seek one. All this also severely damaged (or perhaps more accurately, demonstrated the existing damage to) NATO.

The Future

The divisions across the Atlantic seem likely to remain very great. Efforts to heal the rifts are likely to be palliatives rather than cures that go to the roots of the matter. However, the advantages of, indeed the need for, coherent and cohesive action, whether on the environment, on terrorism, or on international development, remain. Many urgent problems in the field of international relations and security cannot be solved by any one nation alone. Even allowing for some divergences of real interests, there is very much that Western nations could accomplish together. The issues include:

- Pursuing a liberal economic order

- Building up the rule of law and strengthening international institutions

- Defusing international tensions in potential flash points

- Engaging with Islam on modernity

- Fighting against international crime, trafficking, terror

- Promoting development of poor countries.

Unfortunately, one has only to list these to see that they are likely to augment the strains in transatlantic relations rather than lead to effective collaboration. While there are some hopeful signs—the United States is doing a little more on development, and there is some collaboration on crime, etc.—there is very little progress on international law, no agenda on Islam (a U.S. Middle East policy is in place that may lead to benign developments but is at least equally likely to cause major upset and long-lasting turmoil in the region), and there have been setbacks to free trade. The faults are not all on one side, and European countries in many cases need to be less parochial. (Paradoxically, for it was in U.S. politics that it originally arose, the term "isolationist" can now more readily be applied to the Old Continent.) European nations need to develop a full range of capabilities for foreign policy, military, diplomatic, policy formulating, and then to engage in the world, not assuming that Asia, the Middle East, and South America are not real concerns for them but can simply be left to the United States. *Europe in the World* has to be the motto.

The old relationships ended de facto with the collapse of the Berlin Wall. They were further distressed by the early years of Bosnia. The cracks were hidden by Europeans and Americans who for different reasons did not wish to acknowledge the change or even that there could be a change. The theologizing on separable but not separate and the primacy of NATO were examples of this;[1] they were part of a desperate scrabble to prevent U.S. disengagement. The underlying reasons for that attempt were far from clear. For some European countries, fear of Germany may have been a factor; a blindness to transatlantic differences of interest seems to have seized others. In asserting the importance of a transatlantic link the Europeans and Americans were not *ad idem*.[2] The bargain had always meant different things to the contracting parties, and the differences were increased by the end of the strategic situation that had led to the relationship in the first place.

Madeleine Albright as secretary of state famously asserted that the United States is the indispensable power. Given the size and impact of the United States there is validity in that, though not necessarily in the sense in which the secretary meant it. If the United States is adamantly opposed to something it may well not happen, though contrary examples could be found. Moreover, many things, particularly of a major military nature, can at present be undertaken only by the United States. It is not the case, however, that nothing can happen if the United States is not engaged. Many useful and necessary things can and could happen if it fell quiet. In many spheres the world could live with U.S. isolationism; that, however, is not what is on offer. The United States is not isolationist. It is in fact unilateralist, with a strong sense of its exceptionalism and a self-appointed vocation as the shining city on the hill but little experience in continual engagement.

For the United States, the essential issue is how it will manifest its exceptionalism. It has two options: to conduct itself as if the rules that apply to others do not apply to it; to act as if it were truly sui generis; or to act as an exemplar, to say that its vocation is to point the way, by example and precept, for others to follow in creating a civil society of states, possibly even a civil society of civil societies. There seems very little sign of the third at present. The country that historically has stressed the rule of laws over men, that domestically is arguably all too much involved with litigation and has embodied a complex system of constitutional checks and balances as a necessary part of freedom, insists at the international level on reserving the right of Americans to act without law, without checks or balances, and indeed commits itself to preventing the emergence of an equal.[3]

There will in future be a transatlantic relationship, or rather several—United States–EU, United States in NATO, United States and France/Germany/United Kingdom—different from the relationships between other parts of the world. However, it is another question whether there will be any deeper or more special kind of relationship than that which arises from a broad coincidence of approach, and whether in some fundamental sense any European country, or group of them, will enjoy a true strategic partnership with the United States that is different in quality from other relationships and will endure over time and through changing circumstances. If any will, national foreign policies, and in due course the CFSP, may be framed on that basis. If not, they will have to be framed on other bases, perhaps with lesser objectives but also perhaps with greater attention to Europe's and European countries' own concerns.

Future transatlantic relationships will be not only different from the ones that existed for the last half of the twentieth century but less intensive. The objective must be to see that each is as substantive as possible. That means focusing on the real issues and the real nature of the problems, not on a fictitious or recollected but long-gone set of relationships. When all that is possible has been done, there may be less cooperation across the Atlantic than would in principle be desirable. That may be regretted, but the aim cannot be to perpetuate or even stabilize the old relationships. The world has changed, they are gone, and we should not be trying to recall them; they no longer conform to the realities. There is now the need to forge a new set of relationships that can serve Europe's current needs and help promote its own interests, as well as those of America.

Fundamental to the relationships will be how long the world remains unipolar. The U.S. national security strategy may set out the aim of preventing the emergence of any rival, but history suggests that in the long term that may not be an attainable objective. Even if it were, there must be doubts as to how stabilizing it would be. There was much comment in the twentieth century on how destabilizing a balance-of-power approach to international relations can be, and lessons, appropriate or not, have been drawn from the entanglements of the powers before 1914. Unipolarity may, however, also be destabilizing in both the same and different ways; as noted elsewhere, China, India, and others are unlikely to rest content with arrangements in which a country with quite a small proportion of the world's population sets the rules and then interprets and applies them. The same sentiment in even heightened form may apply to much of the Muslim world. The results may include both attempts to combine against the United States in order to balance it (which may well not succeed in a military sense) and the feeding of those feelings that have nurtured al Qaeda. To the extent that U.S. dominance comes simply from the facts of economic and political weight, unipolarity may be disliked but tolerated. To the extent that it is a proclaimed objective, it is likely to provoke reactions, not only in Asia but in Europe too, which will neither help the United States attain its ends nor assist the smooth working of the international system. At the very least, if the United States finds itself carrying a big stick it would do well to walk softly. Better would be to work positively for an ordering of things such that neighbors work together on their security within an increasingly law-aided system. Whatever the perceived deficiencies of European statesmen at present, the fact is that the populations of the major European countries, with the possible exception of the United Kingdom, will not support governments that align themselves with a United States that rejects international law and institutions and seeks overt hegemony and unilateral solutions to the world's problems. Democracy and diplomacy can be difficult partners, but setting aside public opinion in Europe is not a long-term option for politicians who wish to be reelected. Faced with Soviet threats, some were prepared to take political risks; in the absence of such compelling factors they will not seek to go against public sentiment. Many aspects of U.S. culture (in the wider sense) will be warmly welcomed in Europe; a commitment to maintaining a unipolar world will not.

Britain's Relationships Special and Natural

The United Kingdom's relations with the EU and its predecessor organizations have from the beginning been fraught with difficulty. The same is true of its relations with the United States during most of the time of the latter's existence, but this latter is not generally acknowledged. Future relationships with both should include a substantial and substantive revision of British vision (or myopia) and policies.

Britain's problems with Europe are in part due to the legacy and vision of empire, and in part to an absence of the formative experiences of defeat and devastation in war that shaped France and Germany. In part too, however, they reflect the pursuit of a relationship with the United States different in kind from all others. In the beginning a Churchillian vision, that pursuit became a national self-deception in an effort to stay at the top table when, objectively, power had departed.

Whatever the reasons, the inclination to pursue a "special relationship" with the United States at the cost of other more immediate and needed relations dictated by geography, economics, and politics should now be put aside. It brings neither great influence over the United States nor a voice in the world that could not be obtained by other means. Indeed it may well hinder both: so long as the United States knows that it will have British support no matter what, it has no inducement to defer to British opinion; so long as the rest of the world sees London as simply a faithful echo of Washington, it will wish to talk to the principal not the lieutenant and will condemn the lieutenant equally with the principal.

Given American power, there is, of course, an argument for joining with it so as to be on its side. That was not felt to be an argument to join France in Napoleon's time, nor Germany in the twentieth century. Of course, U.S. economic liberalism and democracy are much more desirable things than totalitarianism or even authoritarianism. The United States is by historical standards a benign hegemon. However, as Lord Acton famously observed, all power tends to corrupt, and absolute power corrupts absolutely. With effective checks on the United States from neither international law nor other powers it would be expecting more than history has ever seen that it would always do the right thing. The British government's current approach, though it has post-1945 parallels, flies in the face of some 250 years of earlier history. It may be correct, but at least the question should be asked, and then answered only after careful thought.

Quite understandably, the United States will seek to promote its own interests. It may generally do that in a constructive way. However, its interests will not always be those of the United Kingdom, and it has already made very clear that it will not be constrained by international law when that conflicts with its own judgment of its interests. No prudent British government should assume that it can serve its own or wider interests simply by adopting the U.S. position for the present and the foreseeable future. Often it may do so, but that must be the result of strategic thinking about ends and means. Above all, the United Kingdom must make clear that its support is not given automatically. In any case, even if there is substance in an American position, British interests may be better served by paying attention to other substance in other countries' positions; that, after all, is what diplomacy should be about. It is time for the United Kingdom to take the long view—to think about a balance of advantage, to itself and to others. It should also think about what the world would be like were the United States to be left without a proper partner, one that shared the decisions and the risks.

The so-called special relationship arose much later than is often thought; it was much thinner and did far less for Britain after the Second World War than is commonly believed. So far as it existed, it was forged in the exigencies of war and related to that. It has had continuing military and intelligence utility to the United Kingdom, but it has come at a heavy political price. The benefits have been limited in extent and duration; the costs have been substantial—as earlier generations of American statesmen realized when they tried to induce Britain into a more Europe-oriented course. The relationship became in political discourse a substitute for empire. It is now high time that the United Kingdom and its political classes look at what it has brought and what it may reasonably be expected to bring in the future, and to set against the benefits the costs in national interests foregone.

Perhaps Britain should adopt toward its former colony Thomas Jefferson's prescription for the young republic—peace, commerce, and honest friendship but without entangling alliance. What would Britain lose if it did so? What might it gain elsewhere? At the very least, standing ready to join coalitions on their merits, Britain would be satisfied that its interests were being consulted on each decision; it might even find itself being courted by the United States. Military cooperation would still be possible, as would exchanges of intelligence. Certainly, some in Washington might try to run down the intelligence relationship, which would cause serious losses for the United Kingdom. However, if the relationship continues only at the price of British subservience, it is difficult to see that the balance of advantage is positive for Britain. All the intelligence there is, when the country is not under vital threat, can hardly compensate for having no position on the national interest. Meanwhile, with the ending of automatic support, those elements in the United States determined on unilateral action would be deprived, at home and abroad, of the cover and hence political benefits of British agreement, bought at no cost to the United States. For its part, the United Kingdom would be able to do what it judged right and expedient on the particular merits of each case. In short, the United Kingdom should repudiate the newly proclaimed basis for policy of simply being the closest ally of the United States. Let it become so because Washington courts it for what it can bring, and because Americans feel that gaining its support is worthwhile.

Such a change would meet vociferous opposition from some sections of the British press and so from aspects of public opinion influenced by what they read there. It would have significant implications for the shape and capabilities of British armed forces and so disturb some senior officers. On the other hand, apart from the political and diplomatic advantages, a more rational laying out of limited resources on defense capabilities might emerge from a partial turning away from the desire to produce elements capable of integrating with and operating alongside the U.S. forces in high-tempo warfare. It would require political courage of a high order, given the longstanding tendencies of most British leaders since Suez. If change in the presumption of almost automatic support for Washington were linked, as it should be, with a more positive attitude toward Europe, the initial pressures against it would be very great. There would be a need for sustained political leadership of a high order. It has to be admitted that there seems little sign of that on the horizon at the moment.

As regards Europe, the European Union must mature as a military and political actor, making available the necessary resources and fostering a sense of its worth. The United Kingdom will have to face many problems, some of its own making in finding a place at the center of a more effective Europe. It must continue to strive in that direction, however, while doing all that it can to increase the diplomatic weight and effectiveness of the EU. It must seek, too, to prevent feckless anti-Americanism or equally feckless anti-Europeanism from paralyzing attempts to make balanced and mutually advantageous transatlantic partnerships.

Both distancing itself from an illusory special relationship and increasing the European Union's influence call for a change in British reflexes and in distorted perceptions of history and international relations. The agenda is hard, and the syllabus of learning difficult, but they should be undertaken now.

Notes

Introduction: Why Another Book?

Epigraph: Robert Calasso, *The Marriage of Cadmus and Harmony* (New York: Vintage, 1994), chap. 1.

1. These observations apply in particular to Western Europe—that is, countries not in the Soviet sphere of influence in the Cold War—but they are becoming relevant also to many Eastern European states.

2. That did not, of course, prevent serious differences rising, and, in the earlier years, real threats of things unraveling. For example, in 1953 Dulles, the American secretary of state, warned publicly of a possible agonizing reappraisal of American policy. He told Eden that the United States might swing over to a policy of hemispheric defense, with the emphasis on Asia.

Chapter One: The Beginning

1. President Cleveland stated that the United States itself would adjudicate the boundary and thereafter resist as willful aggression any attempt to assert claims on what it determined to be Venezuelan territory. At the time, the United States had two second-class battleships and twelve cruisers, to Britain's forty-four battleships and forty-one cruisers.

2. In January 1921 the British ambassador in Washington said (to newspaper correspondents) that Britain and America were drifting toward war. His later clarification was that he did not currently foresee an Anglo-American war but did envisage a deadly struggle disguised as peace.

3. That is, cabinet member responsible for finance and economic policy.

4. Certain U.S. actions were decidedly counterproductive. The Smoot-Hawley Act of 1930 raised tariffs to protect domestic industries. The United Kingdom then raised tariffs on most imports, but with preferential treatment for the Empire (and certain other countries).

5. So nerve-wracked did it become that from September 1938 public meetings concerned with international affairs were banned.

6. However, after a speech by a French minister at the opening of an American war memorial in September 1938, which had implied that a U.S. alliance was evolving, he had flatly denied any involvement in a "Franco-British front."

Chapter Two: The Special Relationship Grows and Ends, 1940–1946

1. July–October 1940.

2. From April 1941 the United States undertook the patrolling of the western Atlantic, although formal responsibility for convoy protection remained with the British.

3. After Pearl Harbor, Donovan's organization became the Office of Strategic Services.

4. The British had been intercepting U.S. diplomatic cables in the early days of the war. Churchill was thus aware of Ambassador Joseph Kennedy's advice that making war materiel available to Britain would be a waste of effort.

5. Even then, officials in the United States tried to backpedal and water down the agreement, but the president, Eisenhower, stood firm. As late as the 1990s there were still complications.

6. In fairness to McMahon it must be said that he later declared that if he had been informed by the administration of the history of British-U.S. collaboration on atomic energy he would not have pressed for a bill in so restrictive a form.

7. Prime minister from 26 July 1945.

8. Australia twenty-three thousand, Canada thirty-seven thousand, India twenty-four thousand, New Zealand ten thousand, and South Africa six thousand.

9. At the Placentia Bay meeting in August 1941, which had produced the Atlantic Charter, the tension had already been manifest. The United States had pressed for wording targeted at imperial preference, and the more general political wording on freedom could be seen as anti-imperial.

10. The United States could hope to produce two and a half divisions by September 1942 for operations in the European theater.

11. It is not necessary to accept that the French and British position at Suez was right in order

to conclude that the U.S. position was wrong, both in weakening allies to whom it looked for support in Europe and beyond (and reducing their confidence in the United States) and in not aiding its own position in the Middle East.

12. It is right to note, nevertheless, the intimacy between Macmillan and Eisenhower, which enabled a resumption of cooperation after the debacle of Suez and the (more surprising) close relationship between Macmillan and Kennedy.

Chapter Three: The American Half Century, and European Contrasts

1. In 1919 the Protestant Evangelical Churches of America denounced the League of Nations as the antichrist.

2. They would have wished to see the ABMT retained and certainly not simply abrogated; the CTBT ratified; verification provisions, even if not perfect, for the BTWC agreed; and effective verification implemented for the CWC.

3. Moreover, while successive U.S. administrations were in principle against terrorism, they allowed over many years money to be raised for Irish terrorism and were less than dynamic in pressing for the extradition of convicted IRA terrorists. See the report of the bipartisan (Kean) commission into 9/11, published 22 July 2004.

4. Which is by no means to say that terrorists spring only from the most deprived; many do not. The point is that perceived misery and injustice frequently provoke a resort to violence, especially if no other channels through which to pursue their rectification are felt to be available.

5. In 2003, at constant 2000 U.S. dollar prices and exchange rates, $417,400 million; all Europe $195,000 million; Japan $46,900 million, China $32,800 million, and Russia $13,000 million. Stockholm International Peace Research Institute, www.sipri.org/contents/milap/milex/mex_major_spenders.pdf and www.sipri.org/contents/milap/milex/mex_wnr_table.html.

6. See the *National Security Strategy of the United States* (Washington, D.C.: White House, September 2002), chap. 9, available at www.whitehouse.gov/nsc/nss.pdf.

7. The 2001 fighting in Afghanistan, in connection with a most important U.S. interest, illustrates the favored way of war—on the ground, a handful of special forces and later a few elite

infantry, but engagement of the enemy by local proxies, while the United States provides intense air power. This mode reflects little desire to engage in peacekeeping or state building, essential as they may be to long-term stability.

8. Council of the European Union, "Headline Goal 2010: Approved by General Affairs and External Relations Council on 17 May 2004, endorsed by the European Council of 17 and 18 June 2004," available at ue.eu.int/nedocs/cmsUpload/2010%20Headline%20Goal.pdf.

Chapter Four: The United States and Europe in the Twenty-first Century

1. This view is not shared by all European states. Smaller ones in the east and in the north still see great attraction in U.S. engagement, not least to prevent the domination of larger European neighbors.

2. See, for example, D. Marquand, "Goodbye the West," *Prospect* (August 2004), p. 14.

3. In the area where it is most effective, the economic, the EU has to a large extent sorted itself out. The (supranational) commission has well defined powers and the machinery to apply them.

4. NATO will be similarly affected by its own enlargement and is already suffering from its own lack of coherence and from the unwillingness of many of its European members to be serious about defense.

5. Germany is not yet ready, militarily or diplomatically; European defense without the United Kingdom, Europe's leading military power, is not feasible.

6. See Maartje Rutten, comp., *From St. Malo to Nice: European Defence—Core Documents*, Chaillot Paper 47 (Paris: European Union Institute for Security Studies, May 2001), available at www.iss-eu.org/chaillot/chai47e.pdf.

7. Samuel Huntington had written more than ten years before that a cohesive Europe would have the population resources, economic strength, technology, and actual and potential strength to be the preeminent power of the twenty-first century.

8. GDP 2000: United States $9,764.8 billion, European Union $7,899.3 billion, at 2000 prices and exchange rates; 2004 GDP, at current prices and exchange rates, $11,664.6 billion, EU $12,089.9 billion (all U.S. dollars). *OECD Statistics Portal*, www.oecd.org/dataoecd/48/4/33727936.pdf. The EU

population is 378,000,000, that of the United States 276,000,000.

9. John Winthrop described his intended settlement in Massachusetts as "a city upon a hill."

10. The EU population on 1 January 2004 was 380.8 million, according to Eurostat; that of the ten acceding countries was 74.1 million.

11. Given greater population and broadly equal economic size, European military effort might be expected to be on the same scale as that of the United States. That, however, as well as being unlikely from the European policy side, would seem to run head-on into the commitment in the U.S. national security strategy to avoid the emergence of any potential military rival.

12. The American engagement in the First World War, for example, though important, was small and late. Only with its entry into the Second World War, more than two years after the commencement of the conflict, did it become a major player in European affairs. During the Cold War it provided essential support on the great issue of deterring Soviet aggression, but even then it was by no means always a supporter of the other major interests or policies of European states.

13. See Ewan Harrison, review article in *International Affairs* 80, no. 4 (July 2004), discussing three American-authored books on U.S. primacy and its cost and benefits.

14. See R. Kagan in the *Washington Post*, 5 December 2004, p. B07, available at www .washingtonpost.com/wp-dyn/articles/A34023 -2004Dec3.html?sub=new.

15. Robert Cooper, *The Post-Modern State and the World Order*, 2d ed. (London: Demos, 2000). For a different perspective, which also emphasizes the difficulties, Robert Kagan, *Of Paradise and Power: America and Europe in the New World Order* (New York: Knopf, 2003).

16. "Conventional" here in the sense of normal military, naval, and air formations and weapons, not as opposed to "nuclear."

17. Joseph Nye, *The Paradox of American Power: Why the World's Only Superpower Can't Go It Alone* (Oxford, U.K.: Oxford Univ. Press, 2002).

Chapter Five: Whither Britain?

1. Chartists: members of a working-class movement of 1836–58 concerned principally with electoral reform but associated with a number of strikes and violent confrontations. Martyrs: six members of an agricultural proto-union in the Dorset village of Tolpuddle, who in 1834 were arrested for unlawful assembly and taking "unlawful oaths." Sentenced to transportation to Australia, they were released in 1836 after a public outcry.

2. With the obvious exception of 1933–45. Britain's entry into the First World War was hardly better considered than Germany's; the Powers' failure to get out before 1918 was a common disaster.

3. For example, in 1962 at the time of the failure of SKYBOLT, elements in the State Department, including George Ball, hoped that if it went it would take the special relationship with it, as well as ending the British deterrent.

4. It must be noted the prime minister at least called for proper attention to the conflict and a resumption of processes, and that his pressure led to the president's eventual agreement to the publication of the "road map" and undertaking to press for its implementation.

5. Support ebbed during 2004 in the light both of the difficulties on the ground in Iraq and of the deficiencies in the decision-making machinery that had led Britain into the war. An official report by a former secretary to the cabinet (the Butler Report) made clear serious shortcomings, despite exonerating individuals.

6. It has been suggested that the prime minister (Blair) does not know how to say no to his American interlocutors.

7. As Sir R. Braithwaite has pointed out (in *Prospect*, May 2003), a junior partner who is taken for granted is a junior partner with no influence.

8. D. Keohane, *The EU and Armaments Cooperation*, Working Paper (London: Centre for European Reform, 2002), p. 13.

9. Indeed, the divisions at the beginning of 2003 also caused severe damage to NATO too, though at that stage it was principally France and Germany who were out of step with others in the alliance, especially over protection for Turkey.

10. In all fairness, one should note that Britain has long held back from endorsing the U.S. line on Iran and its inclusion in an "axis of evil." British ministers have also voiced more criticism of Israel than American ones, but that was not difficult.

11. Germany has blocked action too, but with obvious historical baggage that impedes its freedom of action domestically and internationally.

12. Such as who would succeed, by what means, and who would run the country while civil society was being rebuilt, fending off separatist tendencies.

Chapter Six: New Relationships for Old

Epigraphs: George Washington, 1778; George Washington, Farewell Address; and President George W. Bush, State of the Union Address, 2003.

1. For the European Defence Identity. The argument was that there should not be a separate identity or entity but something that could be separated out from NATO. Thus the Europeans would not have a capability divorced from the alliance, its structures, or U.S. involvement.

2. For the United States, NATO was about containing communist expansion, and in due course exerting American leadership over European foreign and defence policies; for the Europeans, it was about resisting Soviet or Russian aggression and safeguarding against German waywardness.

3. *National Security Strategy of the United States*, chap. 9, p. 30.

Abbreviations

EU	European Union
CFSP	Common Foreign and Security Policy
ESDP	European Security and Defence Policy
IMF	International Monetary Fund
NATO	North Atlantic Treaty Organization
NTA	New Transatlantic Agenda
OSCE	Organization for Security and Cooperation in Europe
WMD	weapons of mass destruction
WTO	World Trade Organization

Further Reading

ARTICLES AND PAPERS

Allin, Dana H. "The Crisis of the West." *International Affairs* 80, no. 4 (July 2004), p. 649.

Betts, Richard K. "The Persistence of American Primacy." *International Affairs* 81, no. 1 (January 2005), p. 1.

Calleo, David P. "The Broken West." *Survival* 46, no. 3 (Autumn 2004), p. 29.

Coker, Christopher. *Empires in Conflict*. Whitehall Paper 58. London: RUSI, 2003.

Cooper, Robert. *The Post-Modern State and the World Order*. 2d ed. London: Demos, 2000.

Cox, Michael. "Martians and Venusians in the New World Order." *International Affairs* 79, no. 3 (May 2003), p. 523.

Daalder, Ivo H. "The End of Atlanticism." *Survival* 45, no. 2 (Summer 2003), p. 147.

Dunne, Tim. "Atlanticism in British Security Strategy." *International Affairs* 80, no. 5 (October 2004), p. 893.

Everts, Steven, and Daniel Keohane. "The European Convention and EU Foreign Policy: Learning from Failure." *Survival* 45, no. 3 (Autumn 2003), p. 167.

Hassner, Pierre. *The United States: The Empire of Force or the Force of Empire?* Chaillot Paper 54. Paris: EUI, 2002.

Hopkinson, William. *La fin de l' "Atlantique Nord."* Critique Internationale 15. Paris: Presses de Sciences Po, Avril 2002.

———. *Whither NATO?* Discussion Paper 79. London: RIIA, 1998.

Ikenberry, G. John. "American Grand Strategy in the Age of Terror." *Survival* 43, no. 4 (Winter 2001), p. 19.

———. "The End of the Neo-Conservative Moment." *Survival* 46, no. 1 (Spring 2004), p. 7.

Jones, Erik. "The Rhetoric of Crisis." *International Affairs* 80, no. 4 (July 2004), p. 587.

Kagan, Robert. "The World and President Bush." *Survival* 43, no. 1 (Spring 2001), p. 7.

Kagan, Robert, Bertram Christoph, and Heisbourg François. "One Year After: A Grand Strategy for the West." *Survival* 44, no. 4 (Winter 2002), p. 135.

Keohane, Daniel. *The EU and Armaments Cooperation*. Working Paper. London: Centre for European Reform, 2002.

Leffler, Melvyn P. "9/11 and the Past and Future of American Foreign Policy." *International Affairs* 79, no. 5 (October 2003), p. 1045.

Lindley-French, Julian. *Terms of Engagement*. Chaillot Paper 52. Paris: EUI, 2002.

Lindstrom, Gustav, ed. *Shift or Rift*. Transatlantic Book. Paris: EUI, 2003.

Marquand, D. "Goodbye the West." *Prospect* (August 2004).

Mazaar, Michael J. "Acting Like a Leader." *Survival* 44, no. 4 (Winter 2002), p. 107.

National Security Strategy of the United States. Washington, D.C.: White House, September 2002.

Rhodes, Edwards. "The Imperial Logic of Bush's Liberal Agenda." *Survival* 45, no. 1 (Spring 2003), p. 131.

Rutten, Maartje, comp. *From St. Malo to Nice: European Defence—Core Documents*. Chaillot Paper 47. Paris: European Union Institute for Security Studies, May 2001.

Steinberg, James B. "An Elective Partnership: Salvaging Transatlantic Relations." *Survival* 45, no. 2 (Summer 2003), p. 113.

Wallace, William. "The Collapse of British Foreign Policy." *International Affairs* 81, no. 1 (January 2005), p. 53.

Williams, Paul. "Who's Making UK Foreign Policy?" *International Affairs* 80, no. 5 (October 2004), p. 911.

BOOKS

Blackwill, Robert D., and Michael Stuermer, eds. *Allies Divided: Transatlantic Policies for the Greater Middle East*. Cambridge, Mass.: MIT Press, 1997.

Boyle, Peter G., ed. *The Eden-Eisenhower Correspondence, 1955–57*. Chapel Hill: Univ. of North Carolina Press, 2005.

Charmley, John. *Churchill's Grand Alliance: The Anglo-American Special Relationship, 1940–57.* London: Hodder and Stoughton, 1995.

Colley, Linda. *Britons: Forging the Nation, 1707–1837.* London: Pimlico, 2003.

Cooper, Robert. *The Breaking of Nations: Order and Chaos in the Twenty-first Century.* London: Atlantic Books, 2004.

Denman, Roy. *Missed Chances: Britain and Europe in the Twentieth Century.* London: Cassell, 1996.

Dickie, John. *"Special" No More: Anglo-American Relations—Rhetoric and Reality.* London: Weidenfeld & Nicholson, 1994.

Leonard, Mark. *Why Europe Will Run the Twenty-first Century.* London: Fourth Estate, 2005.

Murphy, John F. *The United States and the Rule of Law in International Affairs.* New York: Cambridge Univ. Press, 2004.

Nye, Joseph S., Jr. *The Paradox of American Power: Why the World's Only Superpower Can't Go It Alone.* Oxford, U.K.: Oxford Univ. Press, 2002.

Ovendale, Ritchie. *Anglo-American Relations in the Twentieth Century.* Basingstoke, U.K.: Palgrave Macmillan, 1998.

Prestowitz, Clyde V. *Rogue Nation: American Unilateralism and the Failure of Good Intentions.* New York: Basic Books, 2004.

Renwick, Robin. *Fighting with Allies: America and Britain in Peace and War.* Basingstoke, U.K.: Palgrave Macmillan, 1996.

Rifkin, Jeremy. *The European Dream: How Europe's Vision of the Future Is Quietly Eclipsing the American Dream.* New York: Tarcher, 2004.

Sardar, Ziauddin, and Merryl Wyn Davies. *Why Do People Hate America?* London: Icon Books, 2002.

Siedentop, Larry. *Democracy in Europe.* London: Penguin, 2000.

Singer, Peter. *The President of Good and Evil: Questioning the Ethics of George W. Bush.* London: Penguin Group, 2004.

Todorov, Tzvetan. *The New World Disorder.* Oxford, U.K.: Blackwell, 2005.

About the Author

Born in 1943, George William Hopkinson read history at Pembroke College Cambridge and entered the Home Civil Service in 1965. Transferring from the Treasury to the Ministry of Defence in 1986, he was appointed head of the Defence Arms Control Unit in 1988 and Assistant Under Secretary of State (Policy) in 1993. As such he was particularly concerned with bilateral relationships with members of NATO and the former Warsaw Pact, European security institutions including NATO, Western European Union, and European Union matters, and negotiations on arms control treaties.

Mr. Hopkinson was visiting fellow in the Global Security Programme, Cambridge, 1991–92. On leaving government service in 1997 he joined the Royal Institute of International Affairs (Chatham House), becoming deputy director and director of studies before retiring in June 2000 to read and write. His particular concerns are transatlantic relations and European security. He has been an associate fellow of Chatham House and RUSI, and a visiting fellow at the Centre for International Studies, Cambridge University. In 2001 he was Senior Visiting Fellow at the WEU Institute in Paris, and in 2003 visiting researcher at Stockholm International Peace Research Institute in Sweden.

His publications include *Changing Options, British Defence and Global Security* (1992), *Whither NATO* (1998), *The Making of British Defence Policy* (2000), *Enlargement: A New NATO* (2001), and *Sizing and Shaping European Armed Forces* (2004). He has also published numerous contributions to journals and to edited works; examples are "Arms Control and Supplier Restraints" in *Non-Conventional Weapons Proliferation in the Middle East* (1993), "International Organizations in the 21st Century: Challenges Facing the International System" in the *Europa Directory of International Organizations* (1999 to 2004), and "La fin de l' Atlantique Nord," in *Critique internationale*, no. 15.

The Newport Papers

China's Nuclear Force Modernization, edited by Lyle J. Goldstein with Andrew S. Erickson (no. 22, April 2005).

Latin American Security Challenges: A Collaborative Inquiry from North and South, edited by Paul D. Taylor (no. 21, 2004).

Global War Game: Second Series, 1984–1988, by Robert Gile (no. 20, 2004).

The Evolution of the U.S. Navy's Maritime Strategy, 1977–1986, by John Hattendorf (no. 19, 2004).

Military Transformation and the Defense Industry after Next: The Defense Industrial Implications of Network-Centric Warfare, by Peter J. Dombrowski, Eugene Gholz, and Andrew L. Ross (no. 18, 2003).

The Limits of Transformation: Officer Attitudes toward the Revolution in Military Affairs, by Thomas G. Mahnken and James R. FitzSimonds (no. 17, 2003).

The Third Battle: Innovation in the U.S. Navy's Silent Cold War Struggle with Soviet Submarines, by Owen R. Cote, Jr. (no. 16, 2003).

International Law and Naval War: The Effect of Marine Safety and Pollution Conventions during International Armed Conflict, by Dr. Sonja Ann Jozef Boelaert-Suominen (no. 15, December 2000).

Theater Ballistic Missile Defense from the Sea: Issues for the Maritime Component Commander, by Commander Charles C. Swicker, U.S. Navy (no. 14, August 1998).

Sailing New Seas, by Admiral J. Paul Reason, U.S. Navy, with David G. Freymann (no. 13, March 1998).

What Color Helmet? Reforming Security Council Peacekeeping Mandates, by Myron H. Nordquist (no. 12, August 1997).

The International Legal Ramifications of United States Counter-Proliferation Strategy: Problems and Prospects, by Frank Gibson Goldman (no. 11, April 1997).

Chaos Theory: The Essentials for Military Applications, by Major Glenn E. James, U.S. Air Force (no. 10, October 1996).

A Doctrine Reader: The Navies of the United States, Great Britain, France, Italy, and Spain, by James J. Tritten and Vice Admiral Luigi Donolo, Italian Navy (Retired) (no. 9, December 1995).

Physics and Metaphysics of Deterrence: The British Approach, by Myron A. Greenberg (no. 8, December 1994).

Mission in the East: The Building of an Army in a Democracy in the New German States, by Colonel Mark E. Victorson, U.S. Army (no. 7, June 1994).

The Burden of Trafalgar: Decisive Battle and Naval Strategic Expectations on the Eve of the First World War, by Jan S. Breemer (no. 6, October 1993).

Beyond Mahan: A Proposal for a U.S. Naval Strategy in the Twenty-First Century, by Colonel Gary W. Anderson, U.S. Marine Corps (no. 5, August 1993).

Global War Game: The First Five Years, by Bud Hay and Bob Gile (no. 4, June 1993).

The "New" Law of the Sea and the Law of Armed Conflict at Sea, by Horace B. Robertson, Jr. (no. 3, October 1992).

Toward a Pax Universalis: A Historical Critique of the National Military Strategy for the 1990s, by Lieutenant Colonel Gary W. Anderson, U.S. Marine Corps (no. 2, April 1992).

"Are We Beasts?" Churchill and the Moral Question of World War II "Area Bombing," by Christopher C. Harmon (no. 1, December 1991).

Newport Papers 4, 10, and from 14 on are available online (Acrobat required) at www.nwc.navy.mil/press/npapers/newpaper.htm.

www.ingramcontent.com/pod-product-compliance
Lightning Source LLC
Chambersburg PA
CBHW072329290526
45794CB00002B/803